THIS IS
HOW

ALSO BY AUGUSTEN BURROUGHS

You Better Not Cry
A Wolf at the Table
Possible Side Effects
Magical Thinking
Dry
Running with Scissors
Sellevision

THIS IS
HOW

Proven Aid in Overcoming Shyness,
Molestation, Fatness, Spinsterhood, Grief,
Disease, Lushery, Decrepitude & More.
For Young and Old Alike.

AUGUSTEN
BURROUGHS

ST. MARTIN'S PRESS ☙ NEW YORK

www.stmartins.com

Design by Phil Mazzone

ISBN 978-0-312-56355-4

First Edition: May 2012

10 9 8 7 6 5 4 3 2 1

For my uncle and aunt, Bob and Relda Robison,
of Dothan, Alabama. With love, gratitude, awe,
and boiled peanuts.

Acknowledgments

I have made many mistakes in my life, and I am, in retrospect, quite grateful for all of them. One mistake I have not made, however, is to take for granted the unwavering support, encouragement, and flexibility of my publisher, St. Martin's Press. I am especially thankful to have had Jennifer Enderlin as my editor from my first book on. She has challenged me endlessly and made me a better, more fearless writer than I ever could have been without her. I am so fortunate to be one of the writers under the care of one of the industry's most respected (and maybe a little feared) editors.

I am also deeply grateful to DPP for all he has done and continues to do for me.

One of the best friends I ever made or ever had in my life died while I was writing this book. Her family's warmth and inclusion of me made this loss no less terrible but so much more bearable. Thank you: D, L, M, and J.

Seamus Mulcare is a wedding cake designer and baker on

ACKNOWLEDGMENTS

the island of St. John, U.S. Virgin Islands, who baked me a cake in the shape of a lemon that turned out to be the best cake I have ever had in my life, and *he* turned out to be one of the funniest and kindest flour-covered people I have ever met. I feel so happy to consider him and his wife, Stacey, friends.

I am indebted to the many people who inspired and then became invisibly woven into the fabric of this book.

A special thanks to Susan King of Melbourne, Australia, whose fierce intelligence, staggering artistry, and innate grace make me wish we were neighbors.

I love you, Christopher Schelling.

To see what is in front of one's nose
requires a constant struggle.

—GEORGE ORWELL

All truths are easy to understand once they are discovered;
the point is to discover them.

—GALILEO GALILEI

How to Ride an Elevator

Several years ago when the relationship I assumed was both nearly perfect and my last turned out to be neither and ended car-off-cliff style, I experienced an unexpected and profound personal *awakening*.

This awakening arrived convincingly disguised as the most miserable and debilitating period of my life—a life that would now be trimmed short from the disease of ruination.

So complete was this state of psychological collapse, it even followed me into elevators.

As I stood in a hotel elevator one afternoon on my way back to my room, it stopped on that floor with all the conference rooms, where they keep the people with name tags.

One such person stepped into the lift, pushed the button for her floor, then took a step back and angled her body so that she was not quite facing me, but neither was she looking straight ahead at the seam where the doors meet, as common American Elevator Etiquette dictates.

Even out of the corner of my now suspicious eye I was able to register the "I'm a people person" body language such a stance suggested.

No sooner had I formed the silent thought, "God, a *people person*. She better not speak to—" I heard this: "It's not *that* bad."

I'd been scrupulously careful to keep my thought about her to myself; she had not done the same.

What's more, she'd spoken these words much louder and with more conviction than you would think necessary for a space roughly the size of four caskets standing on end.

"I'm sorry?" I said.

She was looking at me with an expression of incredulity mixed with boldness. The highlights in her spiky hair had a greenish cast in the unflattering elevator lighting and her lipstick provided her with an upper lip that I saw she did not actually possess.

"I said, it's not that bad," and she gave me that frank, eyebrows up, let's-be-real-here, look. "Whatever it is that happened, it can't possibly be as bad as it looks on your face. How 'bout trying on a smile for size. And if you're all out, I've got one you can borrow."

My first thought was, "It's leaking out of me? People can see it?"

My second thought was, *"Die, bitch."*

But I am much too polite to say something like that so I said, "I'll try."

Encouraged, she continued. "It'll lift your spirits. The first thing I do every morning is smile at myself in the mirror and say, 'You are a powerful, positive person and nothing can get you down today.'"

Thank God the elevator doors were already open and she

was on her way out as she finished yammering at me, but just to be on the safe side I reached forward and began stabbing the Door Close button.

Now, I have an uncommonly high threshold for most any category of stimulation you can think of, but especially when it comes to being shocked, horrified, or enraged.

I was all of these things now. After a mere elevator ride that could not possibly have lasted longer than thirty-five seconds. Maybe forty seconds, if we passed through some sort of time-expanding warp.

Once in my room I had to think, what the hell just happened there? Why do I hate Lipstickmouth so much?

I am not a spiritual person, as I was in childhood. But occasionally, one event in my life will so quickly be followed by a second event that so perfectly replies to the first, it gives me pause and makes me wonder if I still have my St. Christopher medal somewhere.

Glancing down at my laptop, I noticed the following bold headline in my news feed:

SELF-HELP 'MAKES YOU FEEL WORSE.' *Bridget Jones is not alone in turning to self-help mantras to boost her spirits, but a study warns they may have the opposite effect.*

I immediately clicked on the link and was taken to the BBC's website, where I read the article.

Canadian researchers found those with low self-esteem actually felt worse after repeating positive statements about themselves.

They said phrases such as "I am a lovable person" only helped people with high self-esteem.

The study appeared in the journal *Psychological Science*. . . .

They found that, paradoxically, those with low self-esteem were in a better mood when they were allowed to have negative thoughts than when they were asked to focus exclusively on affirmative thoughts. . . . Repeating positive self-statements may benefit certain people, such as individuals with high self-esteem, but backfire for the very people who need them the most.

No wonder I had found that woman so offensive. Sometimes things *feel* that bad.

Sometimes you just feel like shit.

Telling yourself you feel terrific and wearing a brave smile and refusing to give in to "negative thinking" is not only inaccurate—dishonest—but it can make you feel worse.

Which makes perfect sense. If you want to feel better, you need to pause and ask yourself, better than what?

Better than how you feel at this moment, perhaps.

But in order to feel better than you feel at this moment, you need to identify how you feel, exactly.

It's like this: if California represents your desire to "feel better," you won't be able to get there—no matter how many maps you have—unless you know where you are starting from.

Finally, trained researchers in white lab coats with clipboards and cages filled with monkeys had demonstrated in a proper clinical setting what I myself had learned several years earlier in a rehab setting: affirmations are bullshit.

Affirmations are dishonest. They are a form of self-betrayal based on bogus, side-of-the-cereal-box psychology.

The truth is, it is not going to help to stand in front of the mirror, look into your own eyes, and lie to yourself. Especially when you are the one person you are supposed to believe you can count on.

Affirmations are the psychological equivalent of sprinkling baby powder on top of the turd your puppy has left on the carpet. This does not result in a cleaner carpet. It coats the underlying issue with futility.

If affirmations were effective, a rape victim should be able to walk in her front door following the attack, go into the bathroom, and, with her silk blouse hanging in shredded strips from her collarbones, scratch marks bleeding on her breasts—one nipple missing—and her bangs pasted to her filthy forehead with dirt and dried semen, say to her reflection, "I am too strong and independent to be hurt by negativity. I feel unafraid and powerful. I am grateful for the opportunity I have had tonight to experience something new, learn a little more about myself, and triumph in the face of adversity," and then feel perfectly okay, maybe even a little bit rushy on those feel-good endorphins runners are always going on and on about.

When in fact, what does help the person who has been raped is to chew it up and then spit it the hell out. And by chew it up I mean talk about it, write about it, paint it, make a movie about it, and then be done with it and move on. Because here's the truth about rape: you do not have to be victimized by it forever. You can take this awful, bottomless horror the rapist has inflicted on you, and you can seize it and recycle it into something wonderful and helpful and useful. You can, in this way, transform what was "done" to you into something that was "given" to you in the form of brutally raw material. You can, in other words, accept this hideous thing and embrace it and take complete control of the experience and reshape it as you please. This is not to deny the experience and how devastating it is; it is to accept the experience on the deepest level as your own possession now. An experience that is now part of you. Instead of allowing it to be a tap that drains you, you can force it into duty in service to your creative or intellectual goals.

Many people do not want to admit to themselves or others when they are feeling distressed, anxious, insecure, lonely, or any of the other emotions people feel that exist uncomfortably outside the superupbeat umbrella. So it's chin up and sprinkle, sprinkle, sprinkle.

Should I have smiled when that woman stepped on to the elevator?

"Good afternoon. You must be here for a conference. I hope you're enjoying it."

"Good afternoon to you, too. And I am enjoying the conference very much. Always nice to be out of the office for a change of scenery."

"I hear you. Well, this is my floor. You have a terrific day."

"I will. You do the same."

Is that the scene as it ought to have played? Would an exchange of greasy, zero-calorie pleasantries improve the world?

Is the act of making an effort to remain positive and speak in familiar, nonthreatening clichés better, healthier for us, emotionally?

I don't think so.

Why couldn't that woman just speak the plain truth and say something like, "I don't know what's wrong, but I do know that I've looked into the mirror and seen your expression on my face. And I don't really have a point, I just wanted to say that."

Now, there's nothing nasty in what she said; she wasn't crazy or rude.

It's just that, there was nothing useful in what she said, either. No nutrition at all. Truthfulness itself is almost medicinal, even when it's served without advice or insight. Just hearing true words spoken out loud provides relief.

It's not that I wanted her to say something helpful; I hadn't needed her to say a word. What was offensive and kind of vile was that she obviously saw on my face a mood dark and powerful enough to warrant an intrusion.

She then proceeded to both express her disapproval of my mood and suggest I wear a mask that projected the opposite of how I felt.

It was just disappointing that dishonesty was her automatic response to my obvious unhappiness.

In our superpositive society, we have an unspoken zero-tolerance policy for negativity.

Beneath the catchall of *negativity* is basically everything that isn't superpositive.

Seriously, who among us is having a Great! day every day? Who feels Terrific, thanks! all the time?

Nobody, but everybody. Because this is how we say hello to one another.

"Hey, Karen. How are you?"

"Hi, Jim. I'm great, thanks!"

It doesn't matter if what we say isn't really the truth because they're not really asking how things are in our life and we're not really telling them.

Just like when somebody sneezes, we don't say "Bless you" because we're worried a demon may seize this open-mouthed, closed-eyed moment and take possession of the person; we say "Bless you" because that's the thing to say.

If you said to a person, "Hi, how are you?" and they told you they were very anxious because they suspected their teenage daughter might be sexually active and this was just not okay, you would probably feel extremely awkward, try to look concerned and empathetic, but also get away as soon as possible by explaining you were late for a meeting.

If you're at all like me, you would suspect the person had some sort of mental illness and from that moment on, you would do your best to avoid them.

Because they answered truthfully the question that you, yourself, asked them.

Please believe me when I tell you that I am not suggesting you suddenly start yammering on about all your problems next time somebody asks, "How's it going?"

I'm saying, wait. Look at this thing we all do without even thinking about it.

I'm also saying, look at this little lie we tell. Do you think there might be others we aren't even aware of?

I'll go ahead and tell you right now, yes, there are others. Some not so much lies as misunderstandings. Or inaccuracies.

In fact, you can be a very honest person and yet not be living a truthful life.

And not even realize it.

This matters because stripping away all the inaccuracies, misunderstandings, and untruths that surround you is exactly how you can overcome anything at all.

Truth is accuracy.

Without accuracy, you can't expect to manifest large, specific changes in your life.

It's not enough to *believe* something is true.

Knowing in your heart of hearts that the world is flat has absolutely no relationship to the actual shape of the planet, which will continue to spin on its spherical ass despite your belief in its flatness.

Because we only rarely have the opportunity to know the full truth about something, we have to try for as much accuracy as possible. Accuracy can be thought of as an incremental percentage of the truth.

Once again, by "truth" I don't mean "your truth" or "my truth" or some stretchy, pliable, and fully customizable definition of Truth that suits our ever-changing needs.

I mean only the in-your-face, ignore-at-your-peril, star-sapphire-bright, no-wonder-therapy-failed, singular, shackle-cracking, like-it-or-not, rock-bottom, buck-stopping, mind-reeling, complete-transformation *factual* truth that resides at the center of every one of your issues and dreams and roadblocks and tragedies and miracles.

This is not the truth you tell yourself in order to not rock the boat, or to smooth things over or keep everyone comfortable.

The truth is humbling, terrifying, and often exhilarating. It blows the doors off the hinges and fills the world with fresh air.

This is why your search for the solution to the problems, issues, and obstacles you're dealing with in your own life must begin with your mouth.

Specifically, the lies that come out of it.

How to Feel Like Shit

WIPE THAT FUCKING SMILE off your face.
Unless, of course, you didn't put it there. If it just happened, great. You can leave it be.

But if you did manufacture that smile to try to maintain a sunny, positive attitude, get rid of it. Put your bitter scowl back on.

And stop standing up so straight.

Instead of trying to alleviate some of the uncomfortable and unpleasant emotions you feel by "trying to be positive," try being negative instead.

You can stand in front of your affirmations mirror if that makes you feel better. But this time, name the actual feeling you feel and not the daisy wallpaper version.

Even if the sound of these feelings spoken out loud is so ugly to your ears. Even if it takes you a long time to find the words. These can be your new *Rosemary's Baby* Affirmations.

This will help you get in touch with how you actually feel.

"I feel hopeless and fat and stupid. And like a failure for feeling this way. And trying to be positive and upbeat makes me feel angry and feeling angry makes me feel like I am broken, like it works for everyone else."

If that's how you feel—however you feel—then you have a baseline, you have established a real solid floor of reference. Even if sometimes you feel more negative than you want to admit or more depressed or lonelier, it's important to observe your feelings instead of trying to manage them or turn away from them.

You can inspect these feelings, individually.

"So why does trying to be positive make me . . . angry?"

You can investigate why you might feel a certain way. See if you can trace the feeling all the way back to the first time you felt it in this context. Anything you learn about your feelings and why you might feel them is potentially useful because you may end up recognizing what it is you need to change in order to actually start to feel better and not merely tell yourself that you feel fine.

Maybe you feel pressure to be positive because so many people rely on your good, fake-positive energy? If that's the case, screw everybody else. You're not a bottle of Valium.

You know, sometimes just giving yourself permission to feel any emotion without judgment or censorship can lessen the intensity of those negative emotions. Almost like you're letting them out into the backyard to run around and get rid of some of that energy. Optimism is pretty much an essential quality if you want to be a relatively happy, contented person. But a positive outlook can't be purchased through a few affirmations thrown against the mirror.

Optimism sprouts from the knowledge that *you* are in

control of your own life, not your past and not those around you. Part of being in control is taking responsibility for how you feel. This means not just admitting to uncomfortable feelings but then examining your circumstances to see what can be done to change these feelings at the source.

Real optimism is not the pep talk you give yourself. It is earned through the labor involved in emotional housekeeping.

This means asking yourself questions like, are these negative feelings you're experiencing the result of something in your life right now? Or have they been simmering away in your cauldron of mental sickness for years and years?

Negative feelings and behaviors transform over time into compulsions and habits. In my experience, these kinds of feelings need to be broken, not resolved. They have become habits, long drained of their emotional power.

I was angry for many years with a friend, and at a certain point, this anger felt dusty to me. I was tired of looking at it, tired of having it inside me. I did little more than ask myself, "So wait, am I still holding on to all that anger? Really?"

The answer came in the form of a dry sadness, an old sadness. And a resignation. But there was no longer any anger. There was even some compassion.

All I had to do to reach this truth was to ask myself how I felt about the person, in real time, and then listen for the answer.

Sometimes, people avoid recognizing how they feel because they believe the feelings are a part of them, and admitting to harboring anger or jealousy feels like admitting to a physical flaw. So certain feelings are denied. Which is something like believing your house is clean as long as you don't peek under the beds.

But feelings, no matter how strong or "ugly," are not a part of who you are. They are the radio stations your mind listens to if you don't give it something better to do. Feelings are fluid and dynamic; they change frequently.

Feelings are something you *have*, not something you *are*. Like physical beauty, a cold sore, or an opinion.

Admitting you feel rage or terrible pain or regret or some old, rotten blame does not mean these feelings are part of who you are as a person. What these feelings mean is, you need to change your thinking to be free of them. Maybe you need to stop fiddling with an old wound and stirring up these old feelings.

It may be frightening at first to allow your true feelings to the surface; it may even feel dangerous. But it's much more dangerous to your emotional well-being to wish or deny a feeling away.

If your feelings are fresh—say, anger toward a friend—talk about it with them. Keyword: talk. Yelling at somebody because you're angry with them isn't expressing your anger; it's venting it in their face. If you occasionally use a toilet for the purposes of making the whole process of human waste elimination and removal just a little bit more refined, you can also use a more carefully and respectfully modulated voice to eliminate your human anger.

Of course, every now and then, a guy's gotta just piss in the woods or, if he's a city guy, he's got to make do with the sink. So when talking about your anger just doesn't scratch that itch to scream and throw things, you need to not scream and throw things but, instead, see the anger for what it is: fuel. Pissed-off people can accomplish a lot if they don't just spray their rage fuel all over the place but instead use it to power a novel or a business plan or something else productive. This can be done.

There is an instant of choice before the fist explodes into the wall or the face: let it, don't let it. It feels almost like a sneeze—stopping yourself from exploding feels frustrating like a sneeze that won't arrive. But only for an instant. Then, you feel relief that you contained it. Even if the anger is still there.

Rage is a hot, fast-burning fuel. It can be powerful and useful. Or not.

Not to frighten you or anything but if you do happen to feel angry at a friend or even your spouse or partner and you don't express it? The anger will not eventually evaporate. It will ferment into resentment.

Resentment is anger looking for payback. It's also a high-interest-earning emotion. Each new resentment is added to the ones from before. Long marriages have ended in ruin over tiny and insignificant grievances that were never properly aired and instead grew into a brittle barnacle of hatred.

Hatred is clinical-strength anger.

If you feel hatred for somebody you should see a therapist. Not because feeling hatred is abnormal or a sign of mental illness, but because it's powerful and complex. It's also highly corrosive, so without the insulating, protective container of therapy, hatred can eat a hole right through the center of your life.

Frequently, you hate somebody you love or you hate something you want but are afraid to want. Hatred can be made from feelings of rejection or jealousy—powerful emotions. And you don't want to fuck up something important in your life, even if you hate it at the moment. Where there is hate, there should be extra care.

For these reasons, hatred can be extremely beneficial and its acidic properties can kind of scrub your life clean, acting as an abrasive to help you remove indecision and dissolve confinements and limitations. Which takes insight and experience.

All improvements, transformations, achievements, liberations; everything you want to change about yourself and your life; everything you want to make happen, any obstacle you want to overcome, any crisis you must survive—the prerequisite is being able to allow yourself to feel whatever it is you feel and not pretend to feel something you don't.

So the first thing you need to do if you want to truly improve your life, or just survive the worst it has to throw your way, is to go now and stand before your bathroom mirror.

And wipe that fucking smile off your face.

How to Find Love

I

NOT SO LONG AGO, I was at an outdoor café with a
writer friend who was visiting from another city and we
weren't speaking at all. Because we were utterly engrossed in
the conversation between two young women two tables away.

Girl One: "Paula, I try. But to be honest, I'm a little over it.
I mean, I'm kind of feeling now like even if I met him tomorrow, I don't think I would be emotionally available. Because
this whole process has been extremely frustrating to me. I
guess I've reached a place where I'm starting to realize that
maybe I'm not supposed to be with somebody. Maybe I'm
meant to be alone."

Girl Two: "That's not true, that's not true at all. There's totally someone for you. I know it. Your soul mate is out there
looking for you, too. You can't give up."

Girl One: "I've done my part, right? I've put myself out there.

I've worked hard on who I am and on taking care of my appearance. I have done more than I should have to do. So many people have less to offer than me. I worked way harder than Laura, for example. I made a much stronger effort than she did. All she did was go to a friend's wedding. Okay, that was just chance. Well, what about my chance? That's what I'd like to ask. What about the chance I'm supposed to have? No, I'm over it."

Girl One was just this close—and I'm holding my index finger and thumb like one crumb apart—from storming into God's office and really giving it to him. Or, going over God's head and possibly even getting him fired. Because she was so mad that her life had come without a soul mate. And you heard her, she'd done her part.

Oh yes. This girl had just about reached the outer limits of her patience. In fact, I suspect she had already crossed that line. I would not be the least bit surprised if she is now a multi-cat owner. As my brother once said to an ex-girlfriend's older, single sister, "Well, at this point I think lesbianism might be just about the only option left for her to find a mate."

Of course, those words were spoken many years before it became so fashionable to be a lesbian. Now, I would imagine, one would have to pass an entrance examination of some sort.

In all fairness, it can be hard to forget that life is not actually a prearranged social function, complete with an itinerary, a soul mate, and a money-back guarantee.

Whether through movies or just a general, all-media fusion, many people believe in the concept of a soul mate.

This isn't necessarily a dangerous thing but it can easily veer into that direction. If you're one of those people who is single and doesn't understand why, you might want to ruminate over this for a bit.

A belief in a soul mate is often accompanied by a belief that you will meet this soul mate "when I'm supposed to."

Here now, we're kind of heading into the trouble. "When I'm supposed to," "if it's meant to happen," and similar beliefs suggest there is a paid employee overseeing these details of your life.

On the one hand, such a relaxed attitude ought to be commended.

Except this "if we're meant to meet, we'll meet" attitude isn't *truly* relaxed. So we're not going to commend you for it. This attitude is more passive than relaxed. A passivity born of entitlement.

You are owed a soul mate; this has been promised to you since birth. Everybody knows that. So why worry?

Of course, even if this is absolutely true, are you owed a soul mate who will actually knock on your front door?

I'm of the belief that just being patient and letting "what's meant to be, be" is a crutch and an excuse. I believe such passive thinking is an active roadblock.

The first thing you should do is take a look at your life and then, if necessary, get out of your own way.

Early in 2010, *Science* magazine published the results of a study that analyzed cell phone data and declared that "it may be possible to predict human movement patterns and location up to 93 percent of the time" because most of the people studied "seemed to stick to the same small area, a radius of six miles or less."

Isn't that interesting? I thought it was. The same research also said that people who are frequent travelers tended to remain within the same patterns as well.

So when it comes to searching far and wide to find that

special someone, your cell phone says you're not traveling very far or very wide at all.

Keep that information handy while we talk about dry cleaning for a second. When you drop your clothes off to be cleaned, do you go to the same place? I do. There are three or four cleaners all within a block or so of where I live and I go only to one. I don't know if they're the best or the worst of the lot, but they were the first. Being a proper New Yorker myself, that makes them the only.

I'll tell you something else. I moved to this neighborhood first in 1989. The area is called Battery Park City and it's at the southern tip of Manhattan, right along the water facing the Statue of Liberty. If you cross the West Side Highway, you'll be at the site of the former World Trade Center towers, then Wall Street and all of that.

As I said, if you cross the West Side Highway. Which I did in 2010. For the first time. So that only took me one, two . . . twenty-one years.

When I tell this to other New Yorkers they laugh and gasp, "That's crazy! You have to get out more."

But if I ask them, "So when was the last time you walked along the esplanade in Battery Park City?" the answer is inevitably, "Oh, I've never been down there; I hear it's nice."

So even if you think that statistic doesn't apply to you, I bet real, green money that it probably does.

Do you seek out fresh neighborhoods in parts of town you've never seen so you can discover a brand-new dentist every time you need your teeth cleaned?

Once you've dropped off your stained suits at the dry cleaner's, are you really going to rotate your filthy garments among all the local cleaners each week?

When you run out of saltines, are you going to go to the nearest store, or spice it up and head over to the supermarket on the other side of town?

I suspect you go about your daily life more or less as I do: as though clamped firmly to an invisible length of monorail track.

The reason I live in Manhattan is not because I "enjoy taking advantage of everything the city has to offer" like a dubious personal ad; it's because I'm both wasteful and a glutton. I like knowing I have everything right here beside me so I can let it all spoil in the refrigerator next to the broccoli.

Maybe you aren't even aware of how small a geographic circle you live in. But until you stretch your borders just a little, you can't say you've so much as lifted a finger when it comes to finding love. What you've done is wait for love to quit its job, apply for work as a FedEx driver, and put in a request to work on your particular route.

This isn't leaving it in God's hands; this is tying God's hands behind His back.

It's like pacing up and down the condiment aisle at the supermarket and hating on yourself because you can't find a single thing you want to eat. "Oh my God, I can't stand chutney! And *horseradish*? That's for awful old people. This is a hateful store. They hate love here."

It's unrealistic and passive to expect to meet somebody who shares not only your interests and sensibilities, but also your daily routine.

And if you really aren't all that bad and your world is a wee bit bigger than what I'm describing, you still need to get your Napoleon on and take over a little more of the world.

For example, if you take a subway or walk to work each

day, do you ever alter your course? Do you ever get on the wrong train, on purpose?

Because I believe destiny and chance are the oldest poker buddies in town.

You need to go places you have never been and order food you have never ordered and wait in lines you have never waited in before.

If you want to go to the museum on Saturday, go instead to a Little League baseball game.

Once you've opened your world a little, then you need to open your mind.

Because another thing lots of people believe is that they will know the person when they meet them. There will be an instant, profound recognition.

Maybe.

Maybe not.

If you are to be really truthful here, do you think it's possible that over all the time you've been single, every now and then you've fantasized about what it might be like to meet this special person?

Who hasn't done that, right?

Do you think it's possible that each fantasy leaves behind just a little bit of residue?

So that maybe without even realizing it, your brain has kind of formed a visual image of what this person looks like?

If I asked you to—right now, quick—describe the person you will one day meet, even for an instant, does a human form flash in your mind?

If you have such a mental image of the person you expect someday to meet, it could be acting like a coffee filter, automatically catching those minuscule pieces of ground-up insect and Colombian coffee–field mouse tail, shielding your attention from people who do not resemble the blueprint you have generated over time.

I don't believe in the concept of a soul mate. Because we are all unique, but we're also simply too similar.

I think out of seven billion people, there is probably more than just one soul mate. Surely, the paid employee in charge of each person's love life has taken into account the possibility of fatal snake bites and heavy falling objects.

II

Or maybe there's something wrong with you and that's why you're single.

Maybe you're like the guy I had a date with once, who was perfect in every way except for his hair, which looked fantastic and smelled like vomit. I wrote about him in one of my books so I'm consciously repeating myself here, for those keeping score.

Who is going to tell you that your hair smells like vomit?

This is the sort of thing that will ensure you check the "single" box on every application you ever fill out for the remainder of your life.

So, make sure there's nothing like this going on.

Are your teeth weird? A lot of people have really scary teeth. If they all knew they had these teeth, they would fix them. Ask your best friend and say to them, "Tell me the friggin' truth." If you can afford to fix them and you want to, great. But that doesn't really matter because fixing the weirdo teeth isn't what makes them okay. What makes them okay is knowing you have them. And being totally cool with it. Imperfections are attractive when their owners are happy with them.

Are you one of those people who says on a first date, "I'm really not in any hurry to meet somebody, I figure if it happens, it happens"? Because those are the most desperate people of all. I'm just saying this so that if you are this person, you aren't hiding from anybody.

There is no shame in being hungry for another person. There is no shame in wanting very much to share your life with somebody.

It's my understanding that human beings have fairly regularly sought the company of other human beings, pretty much throughout history.

This is, in fact, merely being truthful about what it is we are, biologically: social.

Personal ads and dating websites work. Anything that hurls your ass into the orbit of other living people can work. But there's still a mistrust of the Internet.

A while back, I watched a documentary about suicides and the Golden Gate bridge. During an interview with the best friend of a man who leapt to his death, the friend spoke about how he'd had a conversation with this suicidal guy and the suicidal guy was excited about meeting some woman online.

The friend told him, dude, what are you doing? You're not going to find true love on the Internet. You've got to get out in the world, face-to-face.

I did something I almost never do: I talked back to the TV. I said, "You killed your best friend."

Of course you can find love on the Internet. Exactly as you can find love at the Department of Motor Vehicles, the dry cleaner's, a bar.

Saying, "There are a lot of psychos online. That Craigslist Killer? Yeah, forget the Internet," is just as loopy. Ted Bundy killed college girls. Should you drop out of college just to be on the safe side?

All of these are things you can do that are a little more pro-active than just waiting. Somebody said to me once, "I'm doing the online thing. Most of the people you meet are just totally not right."

The truth is, most people you meet *are* totally wrong for you, whether you meet them online or at an after party for the Oscars. Which is why meeting truckloads of people is almost a requirement. It doesn't matter how many "wrong" people you meet; what matters is doing everything possible to meet that one person. Don't try a new venue—like online dating—thinking you'll meet "better" people; try a new venue because you'll meet *more* people. It's like with diamonds. It can take more than two hundred tons of ore to yield one high-quality diamond. Nobody is obsessing over all this ore; they're focused on that diamond.

Being single isn't a real problem.

It becomes a real problem only when you believe the powers and forces of the universe have conspired against you.

When this happens, you've begun supernatural thinking.

You need to scrape your face against reality. You need to realize that being single when you don't want to be single anymore says nothing about your lovability, attractiveness, or quality as a person. It says volumes, though, about the limits you've established with respect to looking for and meeting new people.

If you're single and you don't want to be, meet more people. It is, in fact, that easy.

III

Then again it could be that meeting people isn't your problem at all. Your problem is keeping them.

Does that sound familiar?

Maybe "they" always turn out to be "assholes" and they never call you again after the third or fourth date.

Maybe it's uncanny how good you are at finding these freaks. But maybe? It's not them.

Maybe you're one person during the first several dates, but then maybe you change into a completely different person once you're more comfortable.

I have definitely done this. I've also wished repeatedly that the effects of Photoshop could be carried over into the real world, for dates.

I just wanted to be the best person I could be when I first met somebody.

This is common. And it's called *lying*.

The best person you can be is the person you are when you are alone on a random Thursday. That's who you are.

When you are on your best "dating" behavior, when you've pulled yourself together and are pretty much the person you plan to be full-time, in the very near future, this is called make-believe.

The desire to impress somebody when you first meet them is caused by a tiny, invisible, freelance divorce attorney who sits on your shoulder and tells you what to do.

Be the person you actually are, not the person you think you should be. The theoretical, vastly improved, Oprah magazine–cultivated New You is a nice weekend project to tinker with. If you want to improve as a person do this slowly, over time. And not all at once, as you sit down at the bar and open your mouth to talk about your true self on a date.

It is much better and wiser to appear on that first date looking as you do in real life with your real friends on a real weekend.

Because here is the truth: if you want to have a chance at meeting somebody with whom you are genuinely compatible, never put your best foot forward. There's no such thing as taking out an advance against your future personality. It never works to go on dates disguised as the person you plan to be.

Never, ever try to impress somebody.

Be exactly the person you would be if you were alone or with somebody it was safe to fart around.

Be that person. Be the person you are right now, alone, reading this book.

And then meet people.

Then hold out until you meet somebody who is utterly impressed.

Because then? You will not have impressed them. They will have been impressed by you.

The difference may seem just a matter of semantics. But it's not. The difference is finding a person who's right for you.

Not one you think is correct.

The other ways won't work. Even if they work for a while . . . they will fail. You will always slide back into being who you actually are. And the person you are with will want a refund.

BUT.

If you meet somebody and they love you when you are

your true, awful, not-ready-yet, boring, not cool enough, not handsome enough, not pretty enough, too fat, too poor self? And if you love them back so much it makes you calm? And they have flaws and you do not mind a single one of them?

That means you get yourself to the church and you pull one of those priests out of bed and you have him cast one of those wedding spells on you. If you're gay and this happens, you just might have to rent a car first and drive to one of the states that operates a few hours ahead.

Because if you found that, you found *it*.

IV

Do you understand that you are exactly attractive enough and thin enough (even if you weigh four hundred pounds) and smart enough and funny enough, even if you cannot tell a knock-knock joke without fucking it up? You are exactly everything enough to the person who thinks you are.

Just like when you look at them, your eyes will get all wet and girly. Because of their beauty. Even if by any ordinary, reasonable standard, they're short and old and have bad skin.

To meet your soul mate, you have to be exposed to other people. And you have to be willing to show them your soul. You have to be only yourself. If it makes you nervous or uncomfortable to do this, good. Even better. Because that's you, too.

You cannot make a mistake on a date with the right person for you.

If you stand up from the table and accidentally trip and the tablecloth along with everything on it lands on the lap of the person sitting across from you . . . if they are the right person?

That will be the moment they realize they love you.

Maybe this happens when you are twenty-three. Or maybe it happens when you reach fifty-four. Or maybe seven days after your eighty-sixth birthday.

Two hundred tons of ore is a great amount of ore. If, after a reasonable amount of time and effort you remain unhappily single, my suggestion is that you employ the services of a cat or a dog.

Both cats and dogs are known hiding places of soul mates.

They are also very, very good at getting strangers to talk to them in kind voices. Which, it should be noted, could be of some use to those who might otherwise be too shy to step forward and say, *hello*.

How to Be Fat

I

I KNOW A WOMAN who has mentioned her weight—and how she needs to lose it—every time I have seen her for the twenty years I have known her.

I have no idea what she weighs but she looks great and her boyfriend is handsome and fascinating and thinks she's hot. She's not skinny. She has hips and boobs and thighs; she looks great, she looks right.

She's an ambitious and successful woman; she pursues what she wants with dedication and focus.

If you spend twenty years trying to get something and you still don't have it, is it admirable to keep trying? Or did you pass admirable several miles back and it's getting close to straightjacket time?

If you are no closer to having something you've been chasing for twenty years, your data is broken. Either you can't get it, period; you already have it; you don't really need or want it; or it's not real.

If this is you and your weight is like a war that you fight with yourself, maybe you should try this: what about not dieting?

If the pressure were off—really off—and you had your own full permission to eat what you wanted, would this make you happy?

When nothing is forbidden, when it's truly perfectly okay for you to climb into bed with a great book, a yellow layer cake from the bakery, and a fork, the cake suddenly has no more street value than the carrot stick. At least after the fourth time you do this. Exotic medical conditions aside, when there is no judgment with respect to what you eat—when you freely and openly allow yourself anything and as much as you please— the calories may add up, but their value to you decreases. The forbidden element is now gone. The rebellion is gone. The treat is gone because everything is a treat so nothing is.

The trick to this is, you can't pep talk yourself into such an attitude and then eat tons of shit, gain weight, and be frustrated because this "not dieting" diet failed, like all the others. You have to let yourself eat how you want to eat for the rest of your life.

It's like buying a really high-quality blue-chip stock for the long-term as opposed to the flashy, sensational bargain that will turn a profit overnight before evaporating.

Almost every serial dieter I know speaks of his or her "relationship with food" and how "complex" it is.

As with any shitty relationship, the solution is not to spend years in couples therapy and scheduling sex every Wednesday. If it's really a shitty relationship, you have to leave it.

If you go on a diet and you lose weight and keep the weight off, that means you wanted it, you got what you wanted, then you actually liked having it, so you've kept it.

But if you diet and fail and diet and fail, you clearly have to stop with the dieting because you don't like diets of any kind enough to follow them.

So. You let yourself eat anything you want and food becomes a commodity. It's less interesting to stand before the glittering, freshly stocked All You Can Eat buffet when you have been standing there every night for the past six months, eating all you want, which is less and less each time. When no food is off-limits, all food becomes equal and calories evaporate, even if they pile on. But these calories, no matter how actually fattening, contain no meaning. Your war with your weight must end because wars require more than one active party.

You could end up actually losing the weight you could never lose back when you were trying like hell to lose it.

Maybe it will take months or even years for this weight to come off. If it happens, it happens as a result of allowing yourself something, not denying. The weight is lost naturally, from a positive mind-set, not manically banished and forbidden to return.

You might not lose any weight at all and this needs to be fine with you.

Unless you have a medical condition or you engage in zero physical activity, your body will try and be the weight it wants to be. It's quite possible your arms and legs and butt will be larger than you have told yourself they ought to be.

The only real authority in the matter is your body. And some bodies are designed to be larger than others. Some people can be quite large and live healthy, very long lives. We're a fat-paranoid nation, but in the data I looked at from the CDC, people who were a little bit larger lived longer and were insulated against certain diseases.

Plus, of all the things you could do with your life, spending so much mental and physical energy on your gastrointestinal tract is somehow too wasteful.

Knowing that you'll feel great about yourself, look amazing, and have so much more fun as a thin person is exactly like believing that being rich would end your financial worries and free you to do things like shop for seven-hundred-dollar vintage T-shirts and finally learn glassblowing. So that you could enjoy life instead of struggling constantly.

No doubt, some things would be better as a skinnier person, just as some things would improve with wealth. But happiness or satisfaction or contentment are not among these things.

Like so much in life, happiness is sold separately.

A more disappointment-resistant plan would be to get "thin happy" now at whatever weight you are. So that *thin* doesn't equal *happy* to you anymore. It's less compelling to obsess over getting more of something you already have.

Losing weight is something you absolutely can do and you don't need a book or a scale to do it.

All you need is *need.*

You must want to lose the weight and become that skinny person more than you want to eat, more than you want the comfort that food provides you. You must want to lose weight to such an extent that the want is transformed under the pressure of your focused and powerful desire into a diamond of pure need.

When want is aimed in a very specific direction, when the want you feel is so strong it's a need, achieving your goal is simple. Not necessarily easy. But simple. And fast, even if it takes a long time. Because when you are focused on a goal, the little steps involved in reaching that goal—such as time—just don't make it onto your radar; they don't matter.

If willpower is required to achieve this goal, that's how you know you don't want it enough on a deep, organic level.

Mechanical failure will eventually occur.

Willpower is like holding your breath: you can only do it for so long.

Which is exactly why willpowering your way through to *thin* won't work. Can you name a single example in your life of when you *ever* needed willpower to get something you really, really wanted, *needed*?

If you are trapped in a car underwater, you will not need willpower to roll down the window. You will feel only one thing: the need for air. You will start trying to roll down that window and either you will roll it down or you will die trying.

Where there is willpower there is a Band-Aid that's eventually going to fall off.

You only need willpower to get what you don't want or you only *want* to want. By want to want, I mean, something you wish you wanted. But don't really.

If you find that you require willpower to lose weight, you aren't ready to lose weight. There you have the truth, as much as you may despise hearing it.

You don't want it deeply and completely enough.

Something within you is reserved in the matter.

This is what you need to solve. You need to know where that voice of dissent is coming from.

For example, maybe you know for a fact losing weight will improve your health and how you feel every day and maybe you have several other really smart, reasonable reasons why you want to get thinner. You know you aren't fooling yourself into thinking your life will be perfect or you will suddenly reverse-age or become beautiful in a way you never were before; you aren't expecting profound changes to your self or your life, except the ones you know you can expect.

But perhaps despite knowing yourself and your motivations as well as you do, you actually find more emotional comfort in food than you are either aware of or willing to admit.

In other words, some other aspect of your emotional or psychological structure is dependent on your continued ingesting of too many calories.

This would be enough to derail your best efforts every time.

When I say that your want must be transformed into a need, I don't mean you can sit with almost constipated focus and effort and *try* to want it more than you already do.

What you can do is level with yourself. Allow the voice of dissent you have stifled to speak.

When you really want something to the point of need, you don't care or even notice the "temptations" that could lead you off course. You don't struggle with cravings, for example. Sure, maybe you have them, but you don't pay any attention to them, so they go away.

Wanting something with every cell in your body makes the effort required to achieve what you want incidental, entirely beside the point. Because your focus never wavers from the goal. You aren't bothered by any distractions because you aren't looking at them—you are seeing past them to what you want in your future.

Unless some part of you is not fully onboard.

Unless some part of you wants things to stay exactly as they are. And no amount of mental sledgehammering is going to change this. What will change it is exploration.

Maybe there is a very good, smart reason why some part of you wants to remain the weight you're at. It could be you haven't been thin since you were sixteen. It could also be that when you think back to being sixteen and thin and happy because you were thin, there was a time when you weren't so happy. A friend of your brother's hit on you in a totally invasive, offensive way. Or a family member commented on your breasts and though it was innocent enough, it freaked you out.

This unexamined part of your mental scaffolding is resisting your weight loss efforts out of self-protection. Sometimes, this concern belongs to a much younger version of yourself. Simply recognizing where this fear comes from, combined with your adult experience, is enough for you to realize fully, "Oh. No, that's not going to be an issue now."

It really can be something that small and old and childlike that's holding you back.

It might also be something else. Only you can discover where this holdout is within you.

And it will be something so close to you, you can't even see it. By close, I mean so intrinsic, so ancient, so much a part of you.

"But I can't be thinner than my sister. She'll hate me."

"But if I do become thin, I might want a different husband, because I settled."

"If I'm thin, I won't have my weight issue as company anymore. I'll be entirely alone. I'll be entirely exposed."

If you can reach the core truth of what holds you back, one

of two things will happen: either you will accept things the way they are, fully. Or you will change into the way you want to be, completely.

When you are in 100 percent agreement with yourself in what you want, you will experience only the sensation of progress.

But what happens if you break down one night and raid the vending machine because there's no other option and you are tired and hungry and frustrated from your nightmare day of travel?

That's just it: you don't break down one night and raid the vending machine. No matter what you feel. It just doesn't happen because the vending machine is not one of the bricks on your path.

It's almost like this: "falling off the wagon," or bingeing, or saying "screw it" to your diet is like one passenger on a train filled with eager, punctual commuters who pulls the emergency string and stops the whole train.

Sure, the train operator can restart the train and continue. But now, nobody onboard has confidence that it will not happen again.

So really, you have to locate that single person—and maybe they're shy and don't want to be found—and you have to tell them they won't be punished but you need to know why they stopped the train.

Because they had a reason.

The difference is, it's not a train; it's your body. And it's not a separate passenger who pulled the emergency brake; it's you.

You need to listen to your full self. Learn the deeper reason why not all of you is in agreement over this losing-weight plan.

II

Maybe the reason you don't want to lose weight enough for the process to be simple is because you feel pressure to be thin, but not desire.

Maybe, in other words, you kind of don't care that much, really.

You think you look pretty good, even if every magazine in the world says you're a fat cow. Maybe you think, yeah, still.

So the wiser section of your brain that would rather be learning Italian keeps throwing cupcakes at you while you panfry your block of soy protein in oil substitute.

Decisions are beautiful. They are evidence of thought and care. Decisions are the polishing cloths of life.

There is absolutely no shame whatsoever in deciding you'd rather spend your life paying attention to something other than the weight of your physical body.

There is no shame in deciding you look fine just as you are. Or even better than fine. There is no shame in deciding to just be fat.

A FEW YEARS AGO, I was at a hotel in Palm Springs, sitting by the pool and writing. A few minutes later, a woman sauntered into the area wearing a sarong, high heels, and a dramatic, over-sized hat. The woman was what one would typically call fat.

I was astounded by her beauty and her utter command of the entire area surrounding the pool. I glanced around at the other people near me and indeed, every man was watching her. Lust is not easily mistaken for repulsion; these men wanted her. The women sitting outside were watching her, too. And their expressions were just as easy to read, as clear as words printed on a white page: how the hell is she doing that?

Because this woman was the sexiest, most sensual woman I had yet encountered in California. I expect the vast majority of those looking at her felt exactly the same way.

How was it possible?

It was possible because this woman saw the truth behind "the truth." She saw that *fat is not hot* is not true.

One day this woman woke up and she put on her jeans and she looked in the mirror and asked herself, as she surely had a thousand times before, "Do these jeans make me look fat?"

But instead of replying to her rhetorical question with a positive, feel-good white lie, she suddenly let out her breath, allowed her stomach to spill over the waistband, and admitted the truth to herself: the jeans did not make her look fat; she *was* fat.

No article of clothing had ever or could ever disguise, conceal, or alter this fact. She was not, by even the most elastic stretch of the definition, a thin woman. She was fat in her arms, fat in her thighs, fat in her stomach, and even her fingers were plump.

III

To stand there in your binding, fattifying jeans before the mirror and proceed to accurately and with great specificity observe and truly absorb what is there . . . the truth can take your breath away.

The truth can also breathe new life into you.

This woman accepted what she saw. Then she said to herself, "Okay. Given that I'm fat but I still want to be magnificently beautiful, I want to be sexy as hell, what can I do?"

And she did these things.

I can't even remember her face. I'm not actually sure if I even saw it. So I don't really know if she was *pretty*.

She was sexy. She was beautiful. She was insanely ravishing. But she could have also been plain.

This is a learning curveball because not only was she fat and hot, she was beautiful with or without being beautiful.

Many clichés are true. "Real beauty comes from the inside" is absolutely one of them. But we hear it and go, "Yeah, so true," and let it slide right past us, unexamined.

You manufacture beauty with your mind.

In exactly the same way certain short people are able to present themselves as tall, fooling everyone. I know somebody who rode on an elevator with Tom Cruise and said, "He was really short but also, he was incredibly tall." This made perfect sense to me.

How to Be Thin

CORNELL UNIVERSITY DID A study and 90 percent of the women they surveyed wanted to be thinner.

So everybody wants to be thin. But apparently, nobody can get there.

Which makes me ask, *what is thin?*

One of the rarest gemstones—and it may, in fact, be the rarest—is a fancy red diamond. While there are plenty of white, black, grey, brown, fancy yellow, and green diamonds to go around, a true, GIA-certified fancy red diamond would sell for well over a million dollars a carat.

The gem is so rare and in such huge demand among gem collectors that this pent-up, frustrated desire is like steam, which propels prices of the stones even higher into the stratosphere.

That's what thin is.

The state of being known as "thin" is sort of the fancy red diamond of human desires.

The desire—and sometimes obsession—to be thin is so elusive that it can support an industry worth over 60 billion dollars in America alone.

If reaching "thin" were effortless or even attainable with ordinary hard work, there would be no 60 billion dollar industry.

Thin would be reduced to quartz crystal.

When something is worth 60 billion dollars, that tells you that almost nobody can have it, whatever it is.

So what is it, exactly?

For some, the desire to be thin actually is a desire for a more slender body. And that's all it is. For these people, getting thin is no more complicated than expending more calories each day than consumed.

For other people, *getting thin* is less a desire than a way of life. A journey that leads a person from one diet right into another. Where the number on the scale each morning is more accurate at predicting whether it will be a good day or a bad one than any horoscope could ever be.

Often, the pursuit of *thin* lasts a lifetime and the goal is never reached.

For these people, thin isn't really about being slender.

Thin is being more beautiful than you are. *Thin* is coming from a wealthier family. *Thin* is a bigger chest. *Thin* is a smaller nose. *Thin* is more followers on Twitter. *Thin* is a more popular channel on YouTube. *Thin* is more friends on Facebook. *Thin* is famous. *Thin* is a perfect score on the SAT. *Thin* is your first-choice college. *Thin* is an iPhone, not a rip-off. *Thin* is having a better singing voice. *Thin* is being from somewhere better. *Thin* is being respected. *Thin* is loving yourself.

Thin may be one of these things or all of them or something else entirely. The reason it's impossible for so many people to ever get *thin* is because what they truly seek is something that can't be microwaved or ladled into a bowl.

In fact, the more obsessed one is with getting thin, the more certain it becomes that one will never get there.

Not even if the physician's scale says you have not only reached thin, you have gone well beyond it. Even then, you will not experience *thin*.

Because your actual desire and obsession is only dressed up in the costume of *thin*. And it's a very good costume; it's fooled you by making you think you don't need to question it. Of course you want to be thin; everybody does.

When everybody believes something, so will you. Unless you pause and think. Maybe you'll still believe what you did before you considered it, but maybe you will feel entirely differently.

I know exactly how it feels to be obsessed with being thin and wanting it more than anything, even though I've never once in my life actually wished to be skinny. But that feeling in me never goes away; it just changes constantly. But it's identical in concept and solution.

If you are insane to be skinny, I can tell you that one day you may very well reach the place you call *thin* and feel so wonderful and satisfied and deeply at peace. I can also tell you that this *thin* you have reached has nothing whatsoever to do with your weight. In fact, you may finally get thin and weigh more than you do now. But the feeling you believe thin will bring you is carried by other needs.

What you have to do is figure those out. You have to figure out what thin actually is to you, what it stands for.

You can do this with a therapist but you can also do it totally on your own. You don't need advice—you need clarity and you need to see the truth. A therapist—or a friend—can some-times say something that is so unexpected, it knocks your brain around and dislodges an insight you had previously overlooked.

Which is how therapy can transform you, but also a friend-ship where you talk, instead of just doing stuff together.

However you can, try and decipher the meaning for you in that extremely loaded word, *thin*.

I'm an alcoholic who doesn't (and doesn't want to) drink anymore so I exist in a state of never-ending micro-addictions that reveal themselves in the form of obsessions. I was the same as a child.

These obsessions are things I want, want to do, or want to be. I become so fixated I neglect every other aspect of my life.

What results is that I get really good at doing a lot of differ-ent things but no matter what I do, it's never the thing that gives me the feeling, *this is what I've been searching for, I am home*. In other words, I never feel *thin*.

One hundred percent of the time.

It's only after causing myself a certain degree of damage that I learn what it was, underneath it all, I was looking for. Once I see that, I can get it. It's usually something within easy reach. It's something basic, elemental.

After I feel it, I might still be really interested in what was before an obsession. Which is like, realizing that thin isn't what you actually want; what you actually want is to *not* feel disliked, like a freak because you have six extra pounds no-body else around you has.

So then you can put your brain in reverse and take a right and start focusing on letting go of the concern you have with how you are—or are not—perceived by others. You can prac-tice not giving a shit.

Which lets the actual *you* out loose, free. This is what causes the feeling, *satisfied*. Or *at home*. Or just *really pretty okay with it all*. All of these phrases describe this feeling.

After you reach it, you might like your weight, you might think you're too skinny, you might think a couple of pounds still need to go but you're cool with that, not crazy over it even if it never quite happens.

That's one of the weird things about some obsessions. To get over them, you have to give them up, let them go, release them, truly not need or want them anymore. Then there it is. It's yours. If you even want it.

In anorexia, something in the brain emphasizes or strengthens the quality of obsession and transforms it into a kind of *punctuated equilibrium*—a biology theory that says, actually most species remain pretty much the same, they don't turn into something else.

So not only is the obsession with thinness exceedingly powerful, it is entirely immovable. It does not change into an obsession with youth or an obsession with career; it's all thin all the time, food none of the time.

It's very difficult to learn about anorexia because it's not as prevalent as many diseases, so it's not nearly as well funded or understood. Which means the treatments are not based on as much science, thus understanding. It's even difficult to name a proper prognosis. The best I could cobble together was this: about half of those diagnosed after age eleven recover. The other half either remains thin—clinically emaciated—or dies.

Fifty-fifty?

A coin toss?

That tells you that this is not breast cancer. I mean, the advances in breast cancer are staggering and brilliantly hopeful.

I knew a woman who lived fifteen years with stage-four breast cancer.

When I was a kid, stage-four breast cancer meant you needed to pick out the outfit you wanted to be buried in.

These are the dark ages of medicine's understanding of anorexia nervosa. So if you have it, you must also cure it.

Anorexia is an extreme. It's like the genetically modified and exaggerated evil clone of *want* or *need*.

Needs and wants: these are helpful things that can be focused and propel you high into your future, into satisfaction with your life.

Need is the focused, highly fortified form of want. Need is want that has been transformed into something closer to certainty by decision and commitment. When you need air, you get it. When you need water, there's no question about what you're going to do: you're going to get a drink even if that means grabbing the garden hose by the neck.

Need can be confused with obsession, but they're very different. Need lacks the dangerous, cycling, all-consuming quality of fixation. When you need something, you get it and move on. But when you're obsessed with something, it's all you can think about.

Obsession and fixation—especially the hyper-obsession/fixation of anorexia—are the emotions of misguidance; they will hijack your brain and destroy your life. You have to break obsession and reclaim your mind.

You have to be like Todd Beamer, the passenger on 9/11's hijacked United Airlines Flight 93 whose last words were, "Let's roll." He and some other passengers attacked the hijackers and brought down the plane, killing everybody—including themselves—onboard and thus preventing the plane from completing its course, into either the Capitol building or the White House.

To break obsession you have to chisel it into pieces. You have to understand the shade of your obsession. How does it make you feel? What is the opposite of this feeling? Did you ever feel this opposite as a kid? Why?

What was happening?

It's almost like hiking, but inside your mind and without a map. I hiked mapless as a kid because we lived in the woods. It was definitely frightening a lot of the time and then it was really exciting and after years of doing it, I was never afraid to explore in a new direction.

Learning about yourself is the same.

Unlike hiking through the unfamiliar woods, learning about yourself is safe.

People always freak out when they contemplate their own damage or baggage because they think understanding the source, seeing the reason, is dangerous and will make their minds explode or something. Or they think they'll end up crazy and in a mental hospital like in *One Flew Over the Cuckoo's Nest*.

But truth is noncombustible.

Yes, it can explode your marriage. If it does, well, it needed to be exploded. Truth will never explode your mind. It will never make you mad.

It will do just the opposite. It will restore you from the madness of a bathroom scale and looking at "68.5" and thinking, "Fat, fat, fat."

If you can freeze that moment on the scale and examine the whole spectrum of how that number makes you feel and what that number makes you want, if you can really try and draw a picture of everything *thin* stands for and means, you then have a chance to penetrate the disease at the deepest and most targeted level.

I believe that the women and men who have successfully overcome anorexia have done so not by taking a pill, recording their daily calorie intake, or measuring their thighs, but by going hiking inside their minds. They learned who they were.

They freed themselves.

By seeing themselves.

It is always safe to see yourself truthfully.

You never have to be ashamed of yourself *with* yourself. All the self-hatred or criticism you may feel in your life doesn't penetrate to the deepest level of you. For some reason, it can't. If it could, most of us would be ruined in childhood.

It is exceptionally rare to be a truly ruined person. Ted Bundy was a defective human. He was ruined.

Nobody with anorexia is ruined.

Everybody with the disease should assume control of their recovery. Take what is useful in treatment, dismiss everything else. Trust your instincts, but not the voice of the disease, posing as your instincts.

Consider yourself.

Let yourself think terrible things about people you love. Let yourself imagine neglecting the needs of those who depend on you.

Do you feel terrible for causing your family so much stress and pain, all because you won't eat? Or do you, secretly, love that you can hurt them so efficiently? Or do you love denying them what they want?

No matter how "terrible" a feeling may seem, it's never terrible to recognize and admit it to yourself.

It's the safest thing there is in the world: *to think your own thoughts.*

Nobody can listen to your thoughts.

God can't listen to your thoughts. Maybe your religion says that God indeed can listen to your thoughts because He, after all, knows everything as the creator of everything. But if there is a God and if this God did create everything and knows everything, He would also know how everything turns out because All There Is already exists whole, within him, so everything happens because it was designed to happen. Which means that I was born to tell you that even God can't hear your thoughts.

So stop being afraid of them.

It's going to be very hard work to fix yourself, but it's much harder work to be employed by an obsession or addiction.

One good thing is that some research into anorexia has actually paid off already. They now believe there is a genetic component to the disease. A predisposition.

Which explains why with all the images we see in advertisements, magazine articles, TV shows, movies—everywhere— do not make all of us anorexic. Only a very small percentage, in fact.

"The media" is generally blamed for if not outright causing anorexia, then certainly being a contributing factor. And it may well be, but only for those with the genetic switch.

If the media images vanished overnight, there would still be people with anorexia; it's been reported in the medical literature since the nineteenth century. It's most likely always existed.

Obviously, superskinny anorexic models are not the only thing that can switch on the gene.

I don't think the media images matter at all, to anybody.

If they vanished tomorrow, tomorrow night something else would act as the trigger.

While you pursue your recovery and assume control of treatment, I suggest you pay attention if something inside you tells you, *this is fucked*.

I spoke to an anorexic teenager girl who is also brilliant and extremely articulate. I was suspicious about one specific treatment, common to most programs: keeping a food diary. That is, writing a detailed record of every food ingested during the day, noting the calories, tabulating the figure.

My instinct told me this was very bad medicine.

This disease magnifies the significance of each calorie. A calorie diary would serve only to show the girl how much she had already consumed. How could she be anything but mortified by the figure—even if a normal eater were to look at her list and be appalled by its sparsity?

I know if I were an anorexic girl and wrote down all the crap I ate during the day and then looked at the total, I would feel so fat and depressed that I would want to immediately diet.

A calorie count on paper would seem like tangible evidence that everything was spiraling wildly out of control.

I asked this young woman how it made her feel, having to keep a calorie journal when she was in the hospital. She said, "It made me decide not to eat another thing."

She decided. At the heart of the illness resides a desire for control.

I tracked back in my own past to a time when I felt that my whole life was totally insane and out of control. I could feel that feeling as fresh as if it were happening all over again. It's a feeling that almost resides in the bladder: you *have* to take action *now*.

Anorexia most commonly affects young women under twenty-five, an age most young people are still under the influence and guiding hand of home or college.

The medical treatment itself, with its highly structured inpatient setting based around mealtimes, therapy appointments, examinations, calorie counting, and supervision, would make a person without control issues feel rather powerless.

But there's more to it than control. When I asked my anorexic friend what she felt when she looked at the scale and saw that she'd lost weight, she said it made her happy. When I asked why, she told me because she wanted to be smaller.

Her choice of words was fascinating. Not thinner, smaller. Thinner means, not as thick. Smaller means, not as much you.

Anorexia is, of course, a disease where one wastes literally away. One shrinks until one dies.

One vanishes.

Control, but more. Something else.

Or maybe not something else.

Maybe anorexia—with its extreme obsessive focus, its never-altering lockdown on one thing: losing weight—maybe these exist in reply to what is a neurological processing disorder with respect to boundaries, authority, sense of self.

Anorexia seems to act as a powerful magnifying lens. I don't know in which or how many ways, but perhaps what a nonanorexic experiences as guidance or advice or somebody else's opinion is warped for the anorexic. Maybe something as simple as, "But first go upstairs and do your homework" is experienced almost physically—as a powerful and oppressive manipulation of behavior.

In the same way that my sensory processing disorder makes the little tag on the neck of a T-shirt feel like the flap from a cardboard box—and it must be ripped away instantly, even if such sudden, desperate yanking leaves behind a hole.

With this connection made, I suddenly knew exactly what I would do if I had a daughter and she was anorexic and none of the prescribed medical and psychotherapeutic treatments had worked. And she wasn't already bedridden and very near death. She'd have to still be mobile for this to work.

I would kick her out of the house.

I would give her a credit card and an ATM card attached to a bank account that held the money I'd saved for her college, along with anything else I had planned on giving her.

I would tell her I loved her. Then I would tell her I was finished raising her. That she would have to take over from now on.

I would explain that I was no longer going to be part of her treatment. I was no longer going to be part of her life. She could be a part of mine, if she wanted and if she made all the effort. But she was free to make no effort at all; I had accepted the loss. I no longer wanted anything from her or for her.

I would say these things even if saying them brought me four inches away from death by heartbreak.

But an exaggerated, magnified—even savagely abrupt— removal of anything that could even remotely be distorted into "guidance" might be the very thing needed to save her.

Maybe someday there will be a pill that lowers the volume in that area of the brain. But there's no such pill now.

The reason we have penicillin today, after all, is because somebody before us was willing to go ahead and eat the blue mold on the bread, to see if it might make the infection go away.

And it did.

How to Feel Sorry
for Yourself

SELF-PITY IS THE BESTIALITY of emotions: it absolutely disgusts people. When you're feeling pity for yourself and somebody says to you, "You think maybe it's time for the pity party to be over? You should stop feeling sorry for yourself and try to think positive," it makes you wish you could saw their head off. Or, at the very least, it pisses you off. But there are probably only seven or eight people in the world who would defend this emotion. So you nod, "I know, you're right."

Self-pity knows it's hated. It's one emotion that lives up to its name: it's something reserved for the self. Self-pity is a feeling you allow when you're alone. If you allow it when you're around other people, they fuss at you and never give you the sympathy you want. So self-pity becomes your private, secret feeling.

Self-pity is what compels you to say, "Oh, I can't this Friday; I have other plans, but thanks for inviting me," when you have no other plans except for spending the evening alone reflecting upon the injustices visited upon you. *"That should have been my parking spot, I saw it before that other car. I'm just saying."*

If you ask somebody, "Why does it piss you off when you see somebody feeling sorry for themselves?" I'm not sure you'd get an accurate answer. I don't think many people have really thought about why self-pity is so offensive.

I'll tell you why I think it hits a nerve.

Remember when you were six or seven? Or if you can't remember that far back, maybe you have a child or a niece this age. But I do remember being six and seven, so I can tell you: it was the most maddening thing in the world to be mistaken for five or six years old. If you were six and a half and somebody dared to call you six, you would absolutely correct them: "AND A HALF!"

At that age, you want to distance yourself as much as possible from babyness. Icky little baby days. You are not a baby anymore.

I believe self-pity is an emotion from our earliest days, probably among the first emotions we experienced.

You can see self-pity every day if you live near a playground like I do. Little kids trip or get shoved and they fall over all the time. Usually, they don't appear to be hurt. They look *surprised* to see that what was just an instant ago beneath their shoes is now pressed up against their nose.

Little kids also know that injuries are an opportunity for extra affection.

So whenever you see a little kid take a spill, they'll look around to verify a nearby adult presence and then they'll let it rip.

This Wail of Death causes all the adults in the area to

converge on the kid and one of them scoops the kid up and begins the medicinal kisses.

Self-pity isn't the most accurate description for this feeling because it describes only half of it: *sad for me, I'm hurt.* What's missing is the other half: *and you need to do something about it.*

This is the infantile half that people find offensive on a primal level. It subconsciously reminds them of when they were six and somebody called them five. In other words, self-pity feels childish to adults. Especially the unspoken but baked-in meaning: and you need to do something about it.

Which is why self-pity is a very dangerous feeling for any adult to harbor.

It's one thing to recognize your hurt. It's quite healthy, in fact, to see and appreciate your own emotional injuries. Especially because as adults, there is no tall, shadow-casting grown-up sitting just within earshot, ready to run to our aid the moment something hurts us. We have to be that adult for ourselves.

Where this healthy self-empathy turns into a malignant self-pity is at the arrival of resentment. "Fuck everybody. Nobody gives a shit about me. Fuck them all."

That is self-pity and it is dangerous because it signals a lack of accountability for one's mental state and, worse, the outcome of one's life. Self-pity can last for years. Sometimes, it can last a lifetime.

In preschool, when somebody hurts us, the teacher sees to it that the person who hurt us apologizes.

It is ingrained in us from a very early age that inflicted pain or wrongdoing or unfairness *should* and *will* be corrected.

Note the passive phrasing: "be corrected." We will not, as children, take control and make sure these amends are delivered in a timely fashion. That is the job of the teacher.

When we learn behavior at a very early age, we forget about ever learning it but the behavior stays with us. Language is a perfect example. Who can remember learning to speak their native tongue? Who can recall their own toilet training?

Yet these learned behaviors have remained with us for our entire lives.

Even if we outgrow them.

In adults, self-pity turns darker and more dangerous as no playground rescue arrives.

The feeling solidifies into victimhood.

Somebody with a victim mentality believes *life* has screwed them over. Somebody with a victim mentality blames everybody else or "them" but takes no responsibility themselves.

This is the quicksand of life. Once you have become a victim, you may very well remain a victim for the rest of your life. Taking no responsibility, no action, and, as a result, seeing no change for the better.

The truth is that nobody is owed an apology for anything. Apologies are lovely when they happen. But they change nothing. They do not reverse actions or correct damage. They are merely nice to hear.

The truth is that life itself is brutally, obscenely unfair. Consider all those other millions of sperm cells that were just as good as the one that resulted in you, and where are they now? Dead, nowhere.

Fairness is not among the laws of the universe. This means, if somebody runs over your foot in a car and they don't stop, that's just too bad and it totally sucks and you better bust your ass to get yourself to the hospital right now so they can save the foot.

Avoid self-pity by taking responsibility for everything that happens to you, even if somebody else is at fault. By taking responsibility, I don't mean play doormat. I mean, repair yourself. Move forward. Move on. Then, only then, see if you can wrangle some empathy.

Most of us have love in our lives. Most of us love other people and are ourselves loved by others.

But make no mistake: you are alone in the world. You were born alone, even if you were born conjoined. And you die alone, unable to bring a single person with you.

Self-pity means waiting for that man with the glass slipper that perfectly fits your foot to knock on your door. Self-pity is waiting to be bottle-fed your dinner.

The truth *behind* the truth is this: even if you are a victim, you must never be a victim.

Even if you deserve to be one.

Because while you wait for somebody to come along and set things right, life has moved forward without you.

How to Be Confident

I

IN ORDINARY, DAILY CONVERSATION most people won't admit to wishing they were less *clingy* and didn't become so depressed when their girlfriend was out of town.

It's unlikely a stranger seated beside you on the plane would turn to you and say, "Do you ever just wish you were more experimental, sexually? What I mean is, do you ever feel like you must be a really boring lay?"

Nearly everyone will freely admit to wishing they had more *confidence*. There seems to be an almost universal shortage of the stuff judging by the number of books, workshops, and websites devoted to the subject.

A common misconception is that confidence arises from *ability* and that if you want confidence, you have to get better at what you do.

This is false.

A person can be utterly incompetent and yet dazzlingly confident. What's more, this same person can know how incompetent they are and still be just as confident. Confidence has nothing to do with ability.

Most of the methods for increasing confidence involve reminding yourself of your past achievements, bringing notes with you onstage if you need confidence speaking in front of others, and repeating positive affirmations to yourself.

All of which seems like kind of mushy advice. But then maybe confidence is a little mushy because, what is it?

How can you really feel like you don't have enough of it unless you really know exactly what it is?

All right, let's start with what it's not.

Confidence is *not* a substance.

It's not like high-density lipoproteins. You can't go to your primary care physician and ask her to run some blood work and check your confidence level because you think it might be low.

Most people would probably say that confidence is a human quality, like compassion or generosity. If this is true, we should be able to describe the feeling, the *sensation* of confidence. There are many ways to describe how compassion feels; it can be an ache of kinship, as one example. Generosity feels something like gratitude and pleasure blended together.

Many people would probably describe confidence, then, like this: "It's just not worrying about whether or not I'll do a good job because I know I will, because I know what I'm talking about."

Or, "It's not being insecure about my abilities. It's knowing what I'm really good at."

But these descriptions actually describe something else.

They describe *competence*.

It is through competence that we feel "not insecure about my abilities." Competence is knowing what you're doing and doing it well.

Confidence isn't competence.

You can know exactly what you're doing and do it exceedingly well, but other people watching you might conclude, for any number of reasons, that you don't look like you know what you're doing at all.

I've known people who were extremely accomplished at something yet nearly paralyzed by a preoccupation with what other people might be thinking of them and how they were being judged. When you're worrying about what people might be thinking, you're distracted. Other people could look at you and see a worried, distracted person, not a confident person.

If confidence isn't competence or a personality feature like compassion, and it's not a substance we can raise or lower by eating more blood oranges, what the hell *is* it? And whatever it is, how can you get more of it *immediately* because now that it's mysterious you need it even more than you did before you thought about it?

The truth about confidence is one of life's wonders because even a lazy person can succeed in this single area: if you want to be more confident, you do not need to add anything more to your personality or your skill level.

In fact, you already have *too much of something.*

Because confidence is not the presence of anything at all. Confidence is a reduction of your own interest in whether others are thinking about you and if so, what they're thinking.

Put another way, to be more confident you need to give a whole lot less of a shit about what other people think of you.

Confidence is not something you feel or possess; it's something others use to describe what they see when they look at you.

The experience others call confidence *you* experience as being at ease, fully yourself, and not self-conscious but rather task conscious.

When you are making a presentation in front of a large assembly of your coworkers or trying to come across well in a job interview, you would naturally want to feel confident in these situations. But trying to feel confident will actually make you anxious. Because you will never experience one instant of confidence in your lifetime.

Instead of even thinking about confidence, what you need to do is focus on exactly what's happening in the instant. Not even the whole moment; the instant at hand.

Only when you are not mentally elsewhere can you be present. And when you are present, you're able to think faster and more creatively and make decisions on the spot. And of course you can do all of these things because human beings have done this for tens of thousands of years. You are hardwired to think, change gears in a heartbeat, come to a decision on the spur of the moment: fight or flight.

By being focused on the task before you—whether it's a question being asked of you in a job interview or a point you want to make to the audience—your mind has a safe harbor. As long as you pay attention only to what is happening right here, right this instant, you will be more fully yourself.

By being focused on the task at hand, you are not focused

on the people around you or their thoughts and opinions. So you don't even have to try to give less of a shit about what people are thinking: this will happen automatically. It's a by-product of focus.

Here's where we have to keep digging all the sand out of the way so we do not lose sight of the truth for one instant: being focused does not mean avoiding eye contact or not making a joke. Being focused means spending time with what you are given as if you were alone or with a best friend.

If you're focused on what's before you but avoiding meeting the eyes of those around you, this is not a fully truthful act.

Being focused on what's happening in the instant during a job interview doesn't mean dryly answering the question, concentrating hard, and looking off into space. That is the behavior of avoidance. It signals anxiety over being judged. It's a lack of focus.

You can't get lost if you just remember to deal only with what is before you and happening right now.

If you are at ease and comfortable—whether or not you're good at what you're doing—those looking at you will see confidence.

Even painfully shy and awkward people are not painfully shy or awkward when they are alone.

The way to access this natural, comfortable alone-self when you are with others is by choosing to forbid yourself to wonder what "they" are thinking. Instead, force yourself to exist in the instant, then take it—and give it—as it comes.

If that sounds terrifying to you, you just cheated.

Forbid yourself to wonder what "they" are thinking.

II

When I was entering adolescence, I was paralyzed by thoughts of how other people were judging me. I was desperately polite. I held doors for everybody and if someone stepped on my foot, I was the one who apologized.

In conversation, I couldn't even form my own opinion because if I admitted liking something the person I was speaking with disliked, I would have felt a profound rejection, like I was left behind.

I could feel this terrible, crushing self-consciousness and do-good best behavior limiting me by the hour. In a moment of mad, brazen inspiration I thought of something I could do that—maybe—would help.

My worst fear, the single thing that made me sick to my stomach to consider was being seen by somebody—especially somebody poised—as rude and ill-mannered. But this fear went well beyond the desire to have fine manners. I had come to feel it was rude to not always accept the blame for everything and to agree with others, automatically.

I simply had to make my worst fears come true. I didn't know how else to stop caring so much about what other people thought of me. If they even thought of me.

I had a very bad idea.

I climbed onto my bike and rode into the next town where there was a corner store I had seen though never been inside.

I would go inside now. But I knew, I would never come back.

As I'd hoped, there were several other customers. I pretended to look at magazines while waiting for a line to form and soon one did. I lost my nerve several times. Finally, though,

I grabbed a pack of gum and cut directly into the line, ahead of two women.

At first they didn't say anything but then one of them politely told me there was actually a line and they were standing in it.

I said something incredibly offensive and stayed right where I was.

Lingering after an act of rudeness terrorism had been my whole point. To stand there and feel their anger and disgust boring into the back of my head. To imagine how the swirl of curls would have infuriated them because when you hate somebody and you're looking at the back of their head, nothing has ever filled you with more contempt than the way their hair brushes the collar of their shirt.

I kind of cheated when I got to the register. The clerk had been oblivious to my crime and I slapped the exact change onto the worn old counter and left before he rang me up.

Looking back? There were probably other, better ways to do this that didn't involve being rude to other people. I'm not proud of this behavior and wish I'd taken the time to think of a different execution of the same concept.

That said, the effect was profound for me.

It became easier to be less involved with other people and more involved in whatever was happening in the moment.

I practiced.

When somebody talked about a movie or song and I felt differently, I started to express this. It was about the song or the movie and how they felt and how I felt. That was all, that was the boundary I established. I did not go beyond this boundary and into the impossible, anxious territory of, "They must think I'm uncool for liking that movie."

The five or six years that followed removed what vestiges of self-consciousness remained. I had felt mortified, humiliated, and degraded in so many different ways and combinations by the time I was nineteen and working in my first job in advertising, the "risk" involved in standing up before people and talking about my idea was laughably negligible.

III

To allow yourself to be "yourself" when you are with others, you don't need to have years of therapy-polished love for yourself—merely tolerance.

When you're on a date or in a meeting or wherever it is you need to be seen as confident or wish you had "confidence," this is the tool to pull from the box and use: be where you are when you're there, doing whatever it is you're doing.

It sounds like advice made out of mist, I know. Just try it in the most literal way possible.

You've got to test drive this concept to really grasp the significance of it. Go walk outside and head to the dog park even if you don't have a dog, or drive over to that creepy Christmas store at the mall that's open all year and lose yourself, misplace yourself, in the moment.

Engage with someone and focus on them, not on your own self, not wondering how focused you are or how much time has passed.

If the lady at the makeup counter offers to spray you with perfume, extend your wrist. Then follow, word by word, instant by instant, the natural path of the moment.

See where it goes.

As long as you don't once look inward but remain focused entirely on the task, you won't lack "confidence."

Until the end, when the perfume spritzer corners you in the parking lot with her box cutter and says she's going to fuck over your face for taking up an hour of her time without buying anything.

But it will be worth it. Because if you are focused on the moment—and this usually means somebody else or some physical activity—you won't be looking inward, judging, quivering at the judgment you have pronounced.

And appearing like a nervous mess without bones or confidence.

Also: this is what will stop you from looking at the wall behind the person you're supposed to be charming during a job interview, FYI.

Think out loud, but don't babble. Babbling is a form of insecurity and anxiety. It's an intolerance for space, silence. Never be afraid of space or silence. They are merely the cool side of the pillow during interaction: a refreshing mental nap.

Delay is deadly. Delay is not a natural pause in conversation. Delay is paralysis, the mind sucking itself out of the moment and grabbing its hand mirror and going, HOLY SHIT, LOOK AT HOW STUPID I LOOK.

Delay is a gun pointed at the temple of confidence. Trying to decide whether or not to say something looks terrible. It looks worse than anything you could possibly say. Even the F-bomb is preferable in a presentation to potential clients than stumbling over yourself and muttering and looking down at the floor like you lost several diamonds.

Saying just the right thing after a considerable, awkward pause is far less effective than saying the wrong thing with perfect timing, I'm telling you.

Worrying about what you'll say means you're out of the moment.

Struggling to find the words to express yourself means you've fallen out of the moment.

You must hang onto the straps of the bucking moment as if your sanity and life depended on it—because actually they do.

Unscripted, unedited, and wholly authentic people are almost universally admired, especially if they have flaws, are not afraid to make live, red-blooded mistakes, and rather than *trying* are busy simply *being*.

Which is something you should consider hiring a tattoo artist to script across the palm of your hand: Be, Don't Try.

"Oh my God, I can't do that. I would totally mess up."

You better pray to the corn god that you do. Messing up is how you tell other people, "It's okay to like me, because I'm just like you." Everybody feels a bit like a dented can inside. Even the slickest, most polished person you can think of is more aware of their shortcomings and flaws than their talents and gifts.

How to Fail

You will learn much more from failing than from making straight As in life. A string of failures is far more valuable than a string of wins.

The reason is that our brains were programmed in the factory to look for and pay special attention to novelty. Which is to say, the unique.

So if you're a straight-A student in school or a metaphorical straight-A student in your adult life, that's a whole lot of the same old, same old.

One A+ paper blends right into the next.

It's when you get a D that you learn something valuable. It's when you fall on your ass that you actually make progress.

I am a complete and total fuckup. Which is exactly why I am equipped to write this book and tell you how to live.

I make rings out of gemstones and bronze and I never went to school for this, I never took a design class and I have no business, actually, handling 1,525-degree metal and chrysoberyl cat's eye gems. But I do it anyway. And when I began, I made one hideous disaster of a ring after another until I had made maybe three hundred.

Each time, I tried to make one nice ring. Each time, I totally failed.

Until ring number 301. Which was suddenly, inexplicably cool.

Now I make more good rings than lousy ones. There are always new mistakes to make. But I almost never make my old, rerun mistakes.

Perfectionism is the satin-lined casket of creativity and originality. If you are a perfectionist, at least stop telling everybody you're one and try to get over it yourself, alone in your home with the lights off.

How to Get the Job

I

ONE OF THE ADVANTAGES of being superior in age to an ordinary twenty-year-old is that I was able to watch the TV movie *Sybil* upon its original broadcast in 1976. For those of you who were deprived of life in this era, *Sybil* starred Sally "My mama always said, life is like" Field as an emotionally troubled girl with multiple personality disorder.

Which meant she could be a hooker one minute and Girl Scout the next and neither one would even know the other existed.

After this movie, everybody suddenly worried they might also be a multiple. How else to explain that pair of two-hundred-dollar shoes you almost don't even remember buying?

Then, meanly, psychiatrists began saying that there was no such disorder. Or, if there was, it was exceedingly rare.

Of course, today we are more evolved and less gluttonous with our psychiatric labels. We know fully well that *dual* personality disorder is indeed a very real thing. After all, anyone who has ever been on a job interview has experienced it for themselves.

You, the rational and reasonable person who is so excellent under pressure could not possibly be the same person who, during the most important job interview of your life, spent the entire interview counting the ceiling tiles behind your potential boss's head.

How absurd to think that was you who momentarily forgot the name of the company at which you were applying for a job.

It's as if there are two of you. The you that you are every day, day after day all your life.

And then the you that you become when you go on a job interview.

My job interview personality also comes out when I am in a store, shopping. I do not shoplift. However, I absolutely appear to others, especially store security personnel, as somebody who does.

Even friends have commented on how weird and guilty and sneaky I look from the moment I walk into a Target.

I am so overly aware of not wanting to be seen as a criminal that I totally come across like one.

It's not such a huge deal when this happens at 7-Eleven. It's pretty huge, though, when you spend the entire job interview trying not to come across like a box of hair and you come across like a box of hair.

As with so many problems, the solution is sitting right in the center of the problem and if you squint you can see it.

". . . trying not to come across like a . . ."

That's the problem.

When you *try* to do or be something, you can't do it or be it.

Because trying is not the same as being. Trying flies in a circle around the moment and *being* is inside of it.

You must be.

You will either do so convincingly and well, or you won't. But at least you will be plugged in to the moment in the process. Not flitting just outside of it, trying to keep everything together like one of those little heel-snapping Sheltie dogs.

Many people get this distinction and want to be in the moment, not hovering somewhere above it. The thing is, how?

By engaging with the person you're with. Which means, not thinking while they're speaking and not forming your answer as they are in the middle of asking the question.

Engaging with the person means following carefully what they say, going for the full ride of their dialogue. So that you don't skip over a nuance by mistake.

This is what'll keep you from zoning out, avoiding eye contact, looking at the wall like a freak, or sweating too much.

During an interview, candor and transparency matter almost more than sheer ability. Skills can be learned, but if somebody is shifty, there you go. They're shifty and can't be trusted, period.

Most everybody is nervous during a job interview. And for the person conducting the interview, it's frustrating because you just wish you could meet the person who would be coming to work every day instead of the job-interview-version of this person, on their best job-interview behavior.

If you had the job, how would you behave?

If the pressure was off, what would you say?

To have or not have the job; high pressure, no pressure: these have nothing to do with sitting in a room across from somebody else in that instant. Getting the job or not getting the job is a conclusion; it comes later. It's outside the moment.

The truth is: You are only the person you actually are; you may not *may not* be the person they actually want.

If you're sitting there thinking, "God, I must look so stupid compared to the other people she's interviewing," you have not reached the truth of what's on your mind.

Thoughts like these are judgments, yes. And they're also beside the point. Forget whether it's "negative" thinking or "a tape" in your mind; it's a fucking daydream. It's not in the room; it's in your head.

Stay in the room. Stay in the instant. Say what you think. But don't let yourself stray from where you are and what you're doing.

II

If you're a stand-up comic and your rent is due so you need the audience to think you're funny, how do you make them think you're funny?

Do you tell them about the seven shows in L.A. that you recently sold out? Maybe read some of the amazing reviews you received?

Or do you tell them a joke and make them laugh?

Because if you actually *are* funny, this would work.

So if you think the job really suits you, *be you.*

III

When you say, "I need more confidence," what you're really saying is, "I need those people over there to approve of me."

That is the desire to control other people and what they think. The first person who figures out how to do this owns the world.

How to Shatter Shame

I

FEELINGS ARE PRETTY MUCH like everything else in our culture: they go in and out of fashion.

In 1983, guys wore shirts with Nehru collars and moussed and blow-dried their hair into a kind of manly bouffant; and they did not say, "I guess I'm just feeling really vulnerable right now."

Vulnerable was not a fashionable thing to be.

That's why everyone wore mirrored shades.

Today, vulnerability is the very height of emotional fashion. It is not so difficult to conjure an image in your mind of a twenty-year-old dude with layered, shoulder-length brown hair, a smear of stubble across his chin, and the innate ability to play guitar, squinting his eyes as he turns away in profile, folds his arms against his chest, and says, "I guess I'm just feeling really vulnerable right now."

Not so easy to imagine is this same guy saying, "I'm really struggling with shame."

Shame is the *Doris* of emotions. It is so out of style that there isn't even any irony in it.

Typically, when something has been dismissed from popularity and sits ignored in the dark past, all that has to happen is rediscovery by a celebrity and whatever it was—hair ornament, make of car, baby name, yoga—is suddenly *it* all over again.

That has not worked for shame.

Because every time a famous person uses the word, it's always in the same sentence: "I have brought shame to my family."

Yet another public relations issue is the somewhat religious overtones the word suggests. This may be partly attributed to the fact that the word *shame,* in one variation or another, appears 235 times in the King James Bible.

It just doesn't seem likely that shame will be the next *cupcakes*. It may be destined to remain terminally uncool, relegated forever to a distant corner of the past we'd rather forget, right there along with clogs.

I have a hunch that this is one big, fat reason why so many people are so fucked up.

And end up spending so much money on psychotherapy, self-help books, and motivational training courses all in search of the ever-elusive *confidence*.

And I told you what the deal is there.

There's just one catch to what I told you: some people find it difficult—or impossible—to focus on what they're doing instead of the people watching. Some people struggle and cannot seem to let go of other people's opinions of them, whether real or imagined. That means they're not able to be themselves. Which means other people won't see them as confident.

This is a *self-esteem issue*.

The phrase "self-esteem issue" is a cardboard stage prop of a phrase. What does it even mean?

I guess I have a hard time believing that anything hyphenated could possibly be the deepest truth of the matter.

A lack of "self-esteem" really suggests a feeling of shame over being one's self.

Shame is the landfill emotion. It's not organic, like joy. It was dumped there by somebody else.

A manipulation.

Shame is very heavy, dense *disappointment*; somebody else's, in you.

Inside of disappointment is a deeper judgment: Less than. Inferior. Defective.

See what I was saying before? Shame can lead to a shitload of problems.

II

Initially, shame is the method adults use to edit children. Shame is a foot that grinds glee into the dirt. It's very effective to say to a child who has just scribbled with crayons all over the wallpaper, "Boys your age don't do things like that, how terrible."

Shame is more coyly deployed by adults in the attempt to modify the thinking or behavior of other adults.

. . .

THE WORD "WHATever," WHEN accompanied by an eye roll, is what shame looks like when you take away its unstylish acid-wash jeans.

What*ever* may be just one word but it shoulders two different meanings that work together to shame someone.

It is a dismissal.

And the eye roll, whether literal or just implied, is a statement of superiority.

But it's a clever, effective statement of superiority because it doesn't come right out and state the position. Rather, the person on the other end of what*ever* concludes it.

If you consider this carefully and honestly, you will notice that if somebody says this word to you, in this way, it makes you feel like a nag, long-winded, tiresome, old, clueless, part of the out group.

Shame is the very height of fashion.

We shame each other at every turn.

And we don't even need a single word to do it.

Fixing a small, straight smile on your face while looking sideways in front of one person and the knowledge that at least a third person sees you do this is shame. You know the expression I'm talking about, right? If you had to add words to it, they would be "Ohmygod, ohmygod, who *is* this person?"

What this says is, "You are inferior to me. And the person here with us? They know it, too. We both know it. You're the only one who doesn't know it."

Shame exists because remote controls for people don't. Shame pushes the button and makes the other person change their channel.

Shame is also a covert and effective bullying method. All those bullies from the seventh grade didn't simply evaporate. They grew up, too, and it's pretty safe to assume that the majority did not seek therapy on their eighteenth birthday to explore their disturbing childhood need for cruelty.

You can't, of course, as an adult make fun of somebody every day at work and expect to keep your job.

So bullies use shame because shame comes in so many different varieties.

How satisfying it must be for the modern bully to locate his target at the office and make remarks like, "Jason, dude, how's it going? Hey man, I'm heading over to the gym at lunch. You know, anytime you want, I would be totally happy to have you come along and I can show you some things you can do, you know, stomach things—make that big boy sit back down flat. Or, a lot of guys, you know, big guys, they get kind of busty. And there's some simple stuff you can do. I would sincerely be very happy to help you out, if you want. I'm just saying."

The shame is disguised here as helpful. But both people in this conversation would know it was bullying.

You can train your eye to identify shame by looking for statements or actions that imply a caste system—"It figures you would like that movie," or disgust—"Okay, I think I've heard enough about your weekend for one morning."

As hard as it is sometimes to recognize shaming language and actions when it's all around you, it's just as hard to know when shame has landed on you.

And that shit builds up.

Because we've been conditioned to accept it since we were kids.

And it happens automatically and fast.

III

Shame also lives inside your head. It's the unnamed voice that says to you:

"God, you are such a slob."

"Look at that fat ass."

"That girl is totally out of my league."

"*Yeah, right.* I'm the next Picasso."

"Maybe I'm supposed to be alone."

Shame says things like that. When you feel spontaneously excited by something—a new career you never thought about, a haircut you see in a magazine and want—shame is the voice that brings you "back down to earth."

"I can't have that haircut. I have too round a face."

"Except I think you have to be really smart to have that job."

Shame often goes in drag as common sense. The belittling putdown that shame speaks in your ear often makes sense because you've likely heard it since you were a child.

"If you keep eating, you're going to get fat."

IV

Dealing with shame is like dealing with a cancer that's spread. There's no single tumor you can remove. No single insight that will cleanse you of the feeling.

What you can do, though, is observe what that inner voice is saying. Is it kind of a nag? Kind of a bitch? Kind of a bully?

If so, it's not you.

If it's not you, it's extra crap. And you shouldn't step on to the plane with stuff in your baggage that you didn't personally pack.

With practice—and it requires practice, like playing an instrument—you can learn to hear the off-key melody of a tape playing inside your head that somebody else put there.

A lot of people *think* they believe things about themselves— not talented, too talkative, too reserved, pudgy, scrawny, average looking, not good at public speaking—because they hear a voice inside their own heads that reminds them of this "fact." If you can pay attention every single time you are hit or stung with feeling, when you feel that weight suddenly fall inside your chest—"Oh. I forgot. I can't sing, I'm not good at it"—stop and examine it.

Did you put that there?

Who did?

Shame is a barnacle that you have to find, then scrape away. Shame is the reason you feel less than, not enough, too much —————————————.

People shame other people because they are jealous, reminded of themselves, recognize in somebody else something they themselves have been taught to hate.

Parents sometimes use shame to expedite obedience. Shame makes you feel bad. It makes you stop what you're doing.

How to See the Truth
Behind the Truth

SEEING THE TRUTH MEANS looking at everything for the first time, every time.

Sometimes, the actual, rock-bottom truth about your circumstances resides behind what you assume is the truth and have never thought twice about.

You must learn to carefully examine both your feelings and the facts and see if you can find yet another door that leads you deeper still.

It's simple. It's not easy.

Blocking your view of what is true is what you think is true—your assumptions, ingrained beliefs, fears, and needs. There can be serious consequences a part of you is not ready to accept if you lift the curtain on what you believe, only to discover the opposite is true behind it.

I recall a woman who struggled for years with intimacy issues with her spouse. She was in therapy to try to learn why she was so uninterested in making love with her husband.

They had, after all, the perfect marriage: they never fought, they were always kind to each other, she didn't trust it at all.

That last part just kind of slipped out in the form of a joke: "It's too perfect to be true."

Later, she would learn of his own deep unhappiness in the marriage, how for the last few years of it he had spent much of his free time planning his own suicide.

In addition, they may not have fought, but plenty about her bothered him. He'd kept a mental list over the years and was able to share some of the things on this list.

It went on and on and on.

Even the fact that she drank diet soda instead of something healthier bothered him and he'd made a note of it.

Hearing this, she felt betrayed. She also knew the marriage was over.

Because she didn't even know this man she was married to. She assumed she did but she had been completely wrong.

The instant she realized this she realized what the sexual problems had been: she'd never been interested in sex with strangers.

Which is exactly what her husband had been: a stranger.

Only she couldn't admit it to herself because to do so would mean her world would fall apart.

It did fall apart.

But she rebuilt it.

Many years later she would read a diary she'd kept from the time when she first met the man. In it she had written that he seemed secretive and there was something she didn't trust.

But she had wanted it to work so she ignored these things.

This is what happens when you go against the grain of truth: you get splinters later on.

Possibly, the real, rock-bottom truth that you need to see in your own life resides behind a similar scrim, which has passed itself off as "the truth" for so long that you wouldn't even think to question it.

In your life, you have a very small, tight bundle of certainties. These are the things that are truly there for you. They may be people, the place you live, your partner, your abilities, maybe even your sobriety. These core certainties are sheltered from your scrutiny. Because you know you can depend on them, you never question them.

That needs to change. You must at least examine them to make sure they're still intact.

One day you may find yourself in an unhappy place where you feel trapped and without options. You may feel you have looked at your situation and realized it's hopeless.

I can promise you that it's not. I can promise you that there is an option and possibly several.

You just might have to move something out of the way first to get a clearer view.

It can be a bit of a puzzle, locating the single aspect of your life that isn't what it appears to be, the belief you assume you hold dear but that, in fact, you've never even questioned.

It's hard to find what you don't know you're searching for.

You have to examine everything up close and look for signs of forgery or those deep scratches that come from forcing something into place that shouldn't be there.

Like a marriage that doesn't contain any sex.

Before you can even begin to heal a sexless marriage, you must know why it's sexless.

I don't need to tell you how dangerous that can be.

Childbirth is dangerous as well.

Heating something to a temperature of eleven thousand degrees is, of course, so dangerous that it perhaps crosses the border into madness.

Which is why we wear sunglasses when we go outside in the summer. Because that's the temperature of the sun.

Dangerous things have to happen sometimes.

Just be careful.

Then make direct eye contact and face them.

How to End Your Life

I

There's always suicide.

Suicide can deliver you to a place of peace and release.
At least, that's what I believed when I was fourteen years old and running scalding-hot tap water over my wrists at the bathroom sink to numb them for the razor blade.

This water-numbing trick had not been my idea; somebody had told me about it, revealed it to me in nearly a whisper, and at the time I had the feeling of sacred, secret information being passed along from conspirator to conspirator. Like having a really beautiful and successful bulimic sit you down and explain, "The reason it's not working for you is because you have to eat your food in colors, right? So have the cake, but follow it with some carrots. So when you puke up the orange carrots, you know where you are and when you should stop or when it's okay to keep going."

It was explained to me that cutting my wrists in the bathtub was by far the best method of suicide and that it wouldn't hurt "hardly at all" if I numbed my wrists first with hot water.

I of course did not think to ask, "How do you know it doesn't hurt? Has anybody ever done this successfully and then come back to offer a report?"

What I did think to ask was, "But doesn't the hot water hurt worse than the razor blade?"

I was told that very hot water burns at first but then almost right away it feels cool. And standing there at the sink quite nearly trembling with an unlikely excitement, as though I was about to load a video game I had waited for since the previous spring, I turned the hot water spigot all the way to the left and I waited until there was a film of steam clinging to the mirror above the sink and then I closed my eyes and lowered my hand into the basin.

I felt a hideous scrape of pain across my knuckles and my instinct was to yank my hand from beneath the faucet and plunge my fist into a refrigerated horse liver; a snowbank would be far too fluffy and useless.

Instead, I repositioned my hand so that the hot water hit the tender underside of my wrist and from this small area arose a sensation so enormous and psychologically overwhelming it could not be described as "hot" or anything other than what it truly was: a room that imprisoned the mind.

Almost instantly, there was a belch of decompression as this stunning sensation beyond mere "hot" became simply a feeling: uncomfortable—now, it was hot—before transforming yet again into the most unlikely sensation of cold.

My fingers began to feel plump and stiff, as though it might be difficult now to make a fist.

And just like that my hand was numb.

It was like an object that my arm bone had decided to carry around—something I was no longer responsible for and didn't have to care about anymore.

I turned off the hot water and turned on the cold and my lip-red hand burned more at this cold than it had at the hot.

I knew then: I can do this.

I can numb both wrists and then climb into the filled bathtub and slice them open lengthwise with one of the razor blades in the medicine cabinet.

My blood would pump, pump, pump into the tub in silky, crimson ribbons before dispersing into a vaporous cloud and turning all the water in the bathtub red.

I would be transported from what to me seemed like the most hopeless and appalling childhood it was humanly possible to have and into a place of release and, ultimately, silence.

I KNEW ALMOST AS soon as I imagined my delivery into this place of release and silence that there could not possibly be such a place.

Peace and release, silence and escape: these were some of the promises suicide made. The problem was, you would have to still be alive to experience the benefits.

The overhead fluorescent lighting of logic had switched on and I saw the design flaw of suicide: if your life is so emotionally painful or empty or just something you desperately need to shed and escape from, suicide is exactly the opposite of what you want because you will still feel these feelings as you angle the corner of the razor blade into your flesh or you curl your lips around the fistful of pills. The steps one must take to initiate a suicidal act and carry it through to completion do not alleviate feelings of depression or provide a feeling of relief; if they did, the suicide would be stopped in progress.

The hardwired human instinct to survive is extremely powerful. It is the reason even the most willful person will not attempt a suicide by holding their breath and then plunging their head into a bathtub.

If the steps involved in executing one's suicide provided one with even the slightest sense of relief or peace or anything at all that reduced the intensity of emotional pain, isolation, hopelessness—if there was any improvement in mood at all, the instinct to survive would plow over the suicidal impulse and the suicide would be aborted.

I saw that in fact, the act of suicide would add—not subtract—to one's feelings of misery. Because even the swiftest method of suicide involves particular steps and is not instantaneous.

If you choose, for example, to cut your wrists in the tub as I had planned to do, once you've sliced both wrists, the suffering that compelled you to reach this moment will now be intensified by what you are about to witness.

Since you were very small you have seen your own naked body in a bathtub innumerable times. To your visual cortex, this is not a novel or surprising image. But once you cut your wrists, the visual center of your brain will instantly recognize a new and unique image and will direct the focus of your mind to this visual. Assuming you've cut your wrists correctly, you will be looking at what resembles two gently pulsing vents, one on each arm, ribbons of blood pumping into the water. Because our brains automatically pay special attention to new information, these pulsing slices will become the largest things in the room.

Your depressive, drunken, or psychotic suffering would now be overlaid with new feelings of horror, awe, fear, and, as adrenaline releases into your bloodstream, the "fight or flight" reflex would engage. This would raise your heart rate and cause the blood to pump into the water even faster. Possibly, you would experience panic.

And yet, at the same time your energy would be draining from you at a rapid speed.

So the last moments of your life would be a very uncomfortable soup of the same suicidally intense emotional pain and suffering, now mixed oil-and-water style, with the desire to flee, confusion possibly, doubt, and, most likely, regret. And this is where you will remain; this is what you will be for the remainder of your life. Inside of this soup.

You will, of course, pass into unconsciousness and death, but you will never be aware of this transition any more than you can be aware of the exact moment when you pass from awake into asleep. For the remainder of your life, you will experience only all the misery that made you want to die plus the horror and discomfort that results from taking the steps needed to end your life.

I realized that "suicide" is just a word, like "kill myself" is a phrase. Words and phrases represent things; they are placeholders. When I speak the word "chair," you likely form an immediate mental image; you know exactly what real-life object I am referring to. I don't need to pick up a chair or point to it to bring it to your attention. I saw that the dishonesty of suicide and all the romantic idealizations that have occurred around it only served to distance one from the brick-and-mortar reality of the physical experience itself.

To see the truth of suicide, you must go through the word itself, which is only a familiar, cushy placeholder for the act, and you must mentally explore and fully imagine—visualize, if you can—each consecutive moment involved in the completion of your suicidal act. It is by doing this that you can see perfectly clearly that no feeling of release or peace is possible.

Even if you select a quick method of death—blowing your head off with a gun, for example—it is not instant. When you mentally follow each of the steps involved in shooting yourself, you will see that even this method is not as swift and trouble-free as you'd like.

The first time I ever pointed a handgun at my head, I was surprised by how awkward it felt because I had to hold it backward. Guns are so carefully engineered to be "safe" that every curvilinear line on the handle has been worked and reworked and focus-grouped and conference-reported to perfection. When you hold the gun wrong, it's unsteady. I discovered this. It seemed to me that it would be quite easy to aim for your temple—believe you had aimed correctly—and instead blow off the top of your ear and a chunk of your temporal lobe and take out the table lamp behind you.

What's misleading about suicide, what I believe is responsible for creating the myth that suicide takes you to a place of peace, is that when the living encounter the body of somebody dead, the absolute stillness of that body is shocking. A dead body does not look like a sleeping body. The first time you see a dead body, it stills you. Never before have you seen a person appear so utterly, perfectly "calm" or "peaceful." We use these words even though they are not quite accurate. They do not describe truly what one sees: the dead person may look calm, but they are not calm; they may look peaceful, but they are not peaceful. They are nothing. They are not.

The word to describe the stillness of the dead has not yet been invented. So we default to words we use to describe living states. And these living states—peace, calm—happen to be states that we all strive to reach ourselves but rarely do for any length of time. When people speak of the dead as appearing calm, their tone of voice reflects their own longing.

Imagine, then, if, instead of describing a dead body as looking calm or, worse, at peace, we said, "Look at her lying there like that. She looks so wealthy."

Substituting those peaceful, romantic, and dreamy adjectives with "wealthy" in the sentence above has an interesting effect. It sounds ridiculous. Why?

Because she's dead.

Except, it's just as ridiculous to say "she looks so peaceful."

The first dead person I ever saw was in a human anatomy and physiology class I took out of curiosity in San Francisco in 1985. In this class, the students had access to human cadavers. One body was assigned to every pair of students. My body had belonged to a young man who overdosed.

When I looked down and saw that young, formerly strong body on the gurney in front of me, I did not think it looked peaceful. My first thought was, "This is a completely new kind of horrible."

If you believe suicide will bring you peace, or at the very least just an end to everything you hate—you are displaying self-caring behavior. You are still able to actively seek solutions to your problems. You are willing to go to great lengths to provide what you believe will be soothing to yourself.

This strikes me as optimistic.

II

There is an option to suicide, albeit an option one should reserve only as an alternative to actually killing oneself because depending on one's circumstances and how completely one takes this action, it can be just as devastating to those who are left behind.

Not everybody who thinks about suicide or actually does it has "reasons" or simply hasn't thought it through. Some people have lost their ability to care about their lives, themselves, or anything at all.

For these people, only a small bump of elevation occurs in mood each day and this is at night, when the sun has finally set and they think, for an instant, "I could go to sleep now, and not have to be awake anymore." But it is a brief bump of elevation, indeed, because this thought is followed immediately by the weight of recognition that going to bed so early will only bring on tomorrow that much faster.

Suicide then isn't always performed in relief of pain—but in a kind of bleak exhaustion as both something to do and a way to block tomorrow from happening again.

The option I'm going to talk about now does block tomorrow from happening again.

Choosing this option will accomplish two things for those who are truly suicidal: it will end their life.

And it will save it.

III

I realized suicide was the last thing I wanted to do. It was actually the opposite of what I desired. Suicide would not accomplish any of my goals:

1. Punishment of those who made me miserable
2. The infliction of lifelong guilt and remorse in everybody who had ever met me
3. Idolization by other suicidal teenagers
4. Something named after me (could be small but not a sandwich)
5. The end of my fucking nightmare of a life
6. Personality transplant

When I saw it this way, I realized something. It wasn't that I wanted to kill myself.

What I really wanted was to end my life.

I hadn't been able to make the distinction before really thinking it through. Ending my life didn't mean I had to die.

It meant I could change my name from *Chris* to something more alphabet-dominant and with numerous syllables, not just the measly one. Something with the subtle sheen of celebrity to it.

Augusten.

As far as last names were concerned, I could toss my father's creaky old rundown *Robison* right into the trash pit. I could pick myself a brand-new last name.

Come to think of it, was there any reason whatsoever I could not name myself after the legendary Burroughs Series E

1400 Electronic Computing/Accounting Machine with mag-
netic striped ledger?

Oh yes. I could. If I ended my life I could start another one.
Where things did not happen to me, but I made them happen.

Just because most people never even think to step outside
their life didn't mean I couldn't do exactly that.

This little speck of Western Massachusetts was the only
place I had ever known. But it was not the only place.

What did I really and truly need in order to be reborn?

Maybe just two things. A door. And then a highway.

I began to feel something flutter, then rise in my chest.
It was the smallest amount of levity. It was the start of that
feeling known as *relief* that I had assumed suicide would
give me.

I didn't need a destination or a plan or even a vague idea of
what I was doing. If it was crazy or rash or insane or irrespon-
sible, then it was all of those things, but it was also *possible*.

Do you know the phrase printed on those fire extinguish-
ers bolted to the wall and locked inside a glass box? The ones
at every school and in every building downtown?

In case of emergency, break glass.

When your life reaches the state of emergency and the only
thing you can think to do is to end it, maybe the thing to do is
break it.

Walk out the door.

So I did.

AS YOU SIT ON your twin bed fanning your courage to just do it
and be done with life, somebody thousands of miles from you
in Goa, India, is carefully, with a sable brush, laying a sheet of

gold thinner than a hair atop a pastry she is preparing for a wedding.

On an island near the equator where it is sunny and warm every day of the year, a young girl with a new pet chameleon in the front patch pocket of her yellow dress is asking her mother, "Mama, what's cold feel like? Is it like wind?"

In Montana or Florida or maybe Detroit, a sleepy old chocolate-colored Labrador retriever who has not been bad one day in his life will be compelled by unknown forces to rise from his spot in the hallway and walk into the kitchen where he will see for the first time in his life a three-tier wedding cake with creamy yellow buttercream frosting and he will allow his tongue to climb over the rim of the plate and wrap itself around a perfect red frosting rose and then speedy quick he'll snatch that tongue right back into his mouth and he will keep doing this until the cake appears to be sitting not on a bed of roses but in pool of dried, smeary blood and leaves.

And in Italy, a seventeen-year-old girl will get a secret tattoo on her left butt cheek and though it will sting for most of the day, it will make her feel ridiculously powerful. Her parents would take her car away or worse, her phone, if they ever found out. But they won't.

This is what I'm saying: you hate your life.

But you don't know what life is.

Life is too huge for you to possibly hate.

If you hate life, you haven't seen enough of it. If you hate your life, it's because your life is too small and doesn't fit you.

However big you think your life is, it's nothing compared to what's out there.

When I lived in San Francisco I knew a crazy lady with a green parrot that suffered from chronic depression.

Oh yes, they can. Parrots absolutely suffer from depression. You haven't met a parrot if you think that's absurd.

Anyway, she was a nice enough lady, considering her madness, and her parrot had a pretty large cage from what I remember. Nonetheless, it sat all day atop its cage looking out the window and plucking its own feathers out.

She had taken it to several animal doctors, each of whom explained to her that parrots were intelligent animals and needed stimulation.

This, she knew. She had lived with it for five years and when it was angry with her, it took her car keys and hid them, so please. Nobody needed to tell her that parrots were intelligent animals.

She was doing what she could to keep him entertained. It wasn't like she could walk over to San Francisco Community College with her bird on her shoulder and enroll him in a semiotics class.

So she did something some people might find quite terrible but that thrilled me.

She opened her window.

That's all she did. She opened her living-room window.

It took that bird like one-tenth of one second to realize the window was open and then he was sitting there on the ledge looking at the huge trees and all the other birds flying around loose.

He flew away.

She knew he would. She had known others who had done the same thing. This was why there are parrots in the trees in San Francisco.

But after several days, the crazy lady woke up and saw her parrot sitting atop its cage, just like always.

She liked to tell the story by adding, "And each day, he would go outside and have his adventures and then return at night. And that bird never hid my car keys from me again."

It's kind of a cool story. Especially if you think life sucks.

Because it doesn't.

It *can*.

But *it doesn't*.

THIS IS THE CHOICE you don't see when you decide to kill yourself. This is the choice that never even crosses your mind. This is the choice that is so obvious, it never even occurs to you.

You can leave. You can open the front door, step outside, and make a right or a left. And keep going.

Yeah, but what about school? What about your wife? What about your kids? What about money? What about all your furniture? What about picking the car up at the shop tomorrow? What about your sister? What about the cows that need to be milked?

Well, yes. It's destructive. But it is a choice. And it's a better choice than suicide.

In a way, suicide is a disease of the eyes. It destroys peripheral vision.

Leaving your life is like getting an intramuscular injection of options.

Maybe this new life will be worse.

Maybe this new life will be better.

Maybe this new life will make you lonely for your old, broken life that suddenly won't seem so broken.

You are allowed to be alive. You are allowed to be somebody

different. And you are allowed to not say good-bye to anybody or explain a single thing to anyone, ever.

The life you have is a life you were given. There were people there already. And a town that had a name. When you went to school for the first time, you did not choose which school.

Some people, though, they'd rather be dead.

Some people can only live if they start over and make a brand-new life, one they make themselves, entirely from scratch.

THERE IS ALWAYS DISHONESTY at the heart of unhappiness. The dishonesty that resides inside suicide is that there are no other options.

So, what about the twelve-year-old girl who is being sexually abused by her stepfather every night and her mother is too drunk to notice or care and there is not another house for miles and miles and nothing of value to steal or sell and she's only twelve, what the hell can she do? All she wants is out and she really does have no options other than the very simple and clean exit offered by the bottle of pills in her mother's top dresser drawer. This girl's life is one endless, awful stinking man's cock and nothing else, not even one tolerable meal a day.

She has options?

She does.

If she strips away all the rules and all she knows and all she sees, she will see the truth: she doesn't have to kill herself. If the highway is thirty miles away and she has no shoes, she can wrap her feet in garbage bags and towels and leave in the very middle of the night by foot.

She can hide in trees if he comes looking, crawl back down when he's gone.

Though she might be bloody and famished, she will make it to that highway.

Adults think, "Oh my God, but she's a baby, she's twelve. She would die in those woods out there alone."

Twelve is not a baby.

Little girls are not delicate, new green ferns. They can be starved, beaten, raped, and beaten some more and not only survive this, but survive it and become black belts in any one of the martial arts so that if somebody tries again to fuck with them, the little girl, larger now, can kill them with either hand.

All children should be loved, protected, nurtured— emotionally and intellectually—respected, and never, under any circumstances, underestimated.

Especially, most essentially, by themselves.

ONCE, A YOUNG MAN told me that he didn't have a mother, she was long gone. And his father was a drunk, volatile, and beastly.

He told me he was gay.

And he was worried that his father wouldn't accept him.

He spoke at some length about why he suspected his father would not accept a gay son.

Then he asked me, what should he do?

I told him the truth about parents, one I myself had learned many years ago.

If you have one parent who loves you, even if they can't buy you clothes, they're so poor and they make all kinds of mistakes and maybe sometimes they even give you awful advice, but never for one moment do you doubt their love for you—if you have this, you have incredibly good fortune.

If you have two parents who love you? You have won life's Lotto.

If you do not have parents, or if the parents you have are so broken and so, frankly, terrible that they are no improvement over nothing, this is fine.

It's not ideal because it's harder without adults who love you more than they love themselves. But harder is just harder, that's all.

I told the young man what I myself had learned when I was even younger than him: parents are a luxury.

I also told him something I did not know at the time: people can change. Parents can change, friends can change, you can change.

While it's true that you cannot change another person, it is also true that you can do or say or be something that inspires them to make the change within themselves.

I told him that if his father rejected him he should accept this rejection for the terrible and painful and infuriating and devastating blow that it is. He should rage and wail and grieve.

And then move clean on forward.

I said, "You can't ever look back and point your finger at this man and blame him for a single thing, not even those things that are his fault. Any damage that's been done, you have to fix yourself because it needs fixing and there is nobody else to do the work. Blame may well be justified but it's not going to move you forward in your life. So don't cling to him after he's taken himself away. There simply isn't that much time in life to waste."

IV

Once you have moved forward, away from the point of assault, the assault slides into the past and becomes a casualty of time's arrow.

Time moves only forward, never back.

We look forward to a moment and then it arrives and an instant later it is gone. Like something on the surface of a river that we reached for but did not touch in time and it carried on, away.

You cannot be a prisoner of your past against your will. Because you can only live in the past inside your mind.

How to Remain Unhealed

I

WHEN I WAS THIRTY-TWO, somebody I loved died on a plastic-covered twin mattress at a Manhattan hospital.

His death was not unexpected and I had prepared myself years in advance, as though studying for a degree. When he died, I was as stunned as if he had been killed by a grand piano falling from the top of a building. I was fully unprepared.

I did not know what to do with my physical self. I could not accept his death at first. It took me about a year to stop thinking, madly, I might somehow meet him in my sleep. Once I finally believed he was gone, I began the next stage: waiting.

Waiting to heal.

This lasted several years.

I had mistakenly assumed that *healed* meant *restored*.

As though scratched by a thorn on my arm, I was waiting

for my flesh to seal itself so completely that eventually there would be no trace and I would forget which arm had been scratched.

It is a terrible thing to wait for something you desperately need that will never come.

I wish somebody had taken me out to the Greek diner on Bleecker Street and ordered for me: Boston cream pie and coffee—just coffee, not cappuccino, not latte. And I wish this person had then simply told me the truth.

Which is terrible but immeasurably less terrible than living suspended inside a misconception for years and years.

I can't give you Boston cream pie or coffee and I'm sorry.

But at least I can tell you the truth about healing. Not the nice, inspiring truth. The real one that almost makes your bones groan to hear, even as you are in some strange way relieved.

Heal is a television word.

It's satisfying to see somebody who has gone through adversity and come out the other side, healed.

That's almost word for word, how they might introduce a segment on healing on a talk show. "Come out the other side." Like a tunnel.

But here's the thing: there are some things in life from which you do not heal.

The tunnel never ends. There is no other side of it.

If your child dies? You will never heal.

What will happen is, for the first few days, the people around you will touch your shoulder and this will startle you and remind you to breathe. You will feel as though you will soon be dead from natural causes; the weight of the grief will be physical and very nearly unbearable. The loss of your child will feel and appear to be something fatal.

Eventually, you will shower and leave the house.

Maybe in a year you will see a movie.

One day somebody will say something and it will cause you to laugh.

You will clamp your hand over your mouth because you laughed and that laugh will break your heart, it will feel like a betrayal.

How can you laugh when your son is dead?

How can you laugh when your daughter is still missing?

In time—perhaps another year, maybe ten—you might have another child.

I'm just saying. *You might.*

To your friends, you will appear to have recovered from your loss. You started over and you have a new family.

What they won't know, however, is that the old family never left the dinner table. All that really happened, you'll think, is that the hole in the center of your life has narrowed just enough to be concealed by a laugh or new son or daughter.

Yet, you might feel a pressure for it to be true. You might feel that "enough" time has passed now, that the hole at the center of you should not be there at all.

You may even feel that by still loving, so much, the dead, you now betray the living.

Maybe there was a lesson you were supposed to learn and, obviously, have not. Maybe this new child will be taken, too.

The pressure to heal can cause enduring damage.

But like losing an arm or a leg in a car accident, no matter what, that arm or leg will never grow back.

II

Parents who have lost a child should be told that they will never heal from their loss. They will always have a terrible, wide hole within them. And other holes, smaller ones.

The way the dead daughter used to smell like apples in the summer? That's a hole.

How the dead boy snorted when he laughed really hard. Another hole.

One hole surrounded by nearly an entire constellation of others.

So no, if your child dies, you will not heal.

Do not wait for the healing to arrive. It will never come. The holes will never leave or be filled with anything at all.

But holes are interesting things.

III

As it happens, we human beings are able to live just fine with many holes of many sizes and shapes.

And pleasure, love, compassion, fulfillment—these things do not leak out of holes of any size.

So we can be filled with holes and loss and wide expanses of unhealed geography—and we can also be excited by life and in love and content at the exact same moment.

Though there will always be days, like the weather, when the loss returns fresh and full and we will reside within it once again, for a while.

Loss creates a greater overall surface area within a person. You expand as a result of it. Though it may well feel like the opposite. If you lose something or someone that is enormously important to you, there can be an overwhelming desire to stop living. To have no new experiences. To shut down.

Huge loss resets you in a way to an earlier time, before you had what it is that you lost. But all you have had, all you have lived remains in you as a part of your structure now.

No matter how huge your loss, as long as you remain engaged with your life, the best days of your life may still be ahead of you.

Don't misunderstand me: the pain of your loss will remain with you for the rest of your life. But great joy will be there right beside it.

Deep sorrow and deep joy can exist within you, side by side. At every moment. And it's not confusing. And it's not a conflict.

This is among the oldest, deepest, most primal truths: the facts of life may be, at times, unbearably painful. But the core, the bones of life are generous beyond all reason or belief. Those things that ought to kill us do not. This should be taken as encouragement to continue.

And when the Worst Thing That Could Possibly Happen is what happens, you would not believe that anywhere in your future exists one of your very happiest moments. What you would believe, and be quite certain of, is that any good days and certainly your best days were behind you now.

But believing something is true, even with all your heart, is unrelated to whether or not what you believe is true.

While there are some things from which you never heal, so be it.

The truth about healing is that you don't need to heal to be whole.

By whole, I mean damaged, missing pieces of who you were, your heart—missing what feels like some of your most important parts. Yet not missing any part of you at all. Being, in truth, larger than you were before.

Because all of us are made not only of what we have but of what we lost.

And loss is not a subtraction. As an experience, it is an addition.

Even when we lose a leg or an arm, there's not less of us but more. Human experience weighs more than human tissue.

Why Having It All Is Not

Sometimes life hands us gift-wrapped shit. And we're like, "This isn't a gift; it's shit. Screw you."

One such gift comes with the wrapping paper known as *limits*.

Oh, how we hate limits.

Limits hold you back. They confine you. They prevent you from doing what you want to do.

Limits stop you from living a life without limits.

Of course, this is only an illusion. What limits really do is give you an acceptable excuse to avoid doing something.

Limits are actually opportunities. Which I know sounds like something printed on a poster in a Human Resources office, but the truth about not having everything you need, not being fully equipped, qualified, or allowed is that these limits are the nebula of creative genius.

Limits force you to make the best of things. And "making the best" of something is a creative act.

It requires a measure of innovation to accomplish something when there are limits blocking the way: a lack of skill, a lack of knowledge, a lack of funds, a limited set of tools. To circumvent the limits you must create a novel solution or find an alternate route.

Limits force improvisation. Improvisation creates new things.

When you have total freedom—no limits at all—you stop trying to make the best of things.

This is the problem with "having it all": there is nothing left to want.

Everything around you is of equal weight.

Value drains away from life and with unlimited freedom you feel not free and drunk with all the possibilities before you; possibilities are rendered into commodities.

I know this because I was raised with the very freedom every adolescent dreams of: no bedtime, no school, no structure, not one single figure of authority to tell me no.

It was great until it was ordinary and then all that freedom was oppressive. Sameness is enormously heavy.

Having a bedtime is good.

Not having it all is good.

Losing something you need or giving it away is also good.

I've known several people who "have it all" and wonder why they feel stagnant in life. When you do have fairly bottomless financial resources, a family, friends, you feel unjustified and spoiled for harboring any sort of dissatisfaction.

I don't believe you can feel deep satisfaction in your life unless your life contains restless areas, holes, imperfections, shit.

How to Get Over Your Addiction to the Past

I

MANY PEOPLE CONTINUE TO feel influenced and even controlled by the things that happened to them a long time ago. Sometimes, people harbor dark, traumatic memories from childhood. Or fragments of memories—incomplete scenes, uncomfortable feelings, perhaps even a sense of certainty that something specific and terrible happened to them, but little more than this.

Others experienced something traumatic in adulthood that continues to affect them day to day many years later. Maybe an assault has left a person afraid to leave their home or enter a particular neighborhood.

For a certain kind of person this will be the end of the story. Whatever experience they endured essentially continues to this day, ever present in the background, shaping the choices made on a daily basis, affecting the quality and range of their life. This kind of person might be angry all the time or feel guilty or afraid. They just accept these states as a part of themselves.

Then there are people who are keenly aware of their experiences, who are psychologically ambitious; they wish to "get over" these historical traumas and might see a therapist to help them.

The therapeutic process takes time, commitment, and funding. Then, insight leads to understanding, which leads to choice. At last, they are free to move on.

It's such a clean, well-defined structure for the process of healing. Almost like a paint-by-numbers portrait where all those black outlines are confusing at first, but in time, as you apply the correct colors in the right areas, the tangle of lines resolves into a perfectly clear image.

Unfortunately, our brains tend to color outside the line.

First, there is the matter of *understanding* our past and the events that transpired.

Understanding what happened in the past is rarely truly possible. Because true understanding must incorporate context. Not merely what we experienced, but why. And the why requires knowing the motivations of the other people involved. Without the perspective of this context, our understanding will always be biased; it will be from a single perspective: ours. And therefore, not necessarily accurate or true.

If you are on a highway and you drive past a car accident so severe that the hood of the car has been crushed up against the windshield, you may very well assume the occupants are dead. And perhaps this will haunt you because as you passed by the car, you glimpsed a little girl's doll on the shelf behind the backseat. One look at that accident was all anybody would need to know what "unsurvivable" looked like. And you have never been able to forget that doll or the little girl who must have loved it and who died in such a terrible crumple of steel and glass. Let's imagine that you are haunted by dreams where you come upon the accident and you see the doll and you do nothing.

Let's say that what was unknown to you was that the car was a high-end Mercedes that featured crumple zones designed to absorb the impact of a crash while protecting the occupants within a safety cage. And let's say that the two occupants inside the car were sitting there as you drove by and the man in the driver's seat was on his cell phone.

"No, I mean totally like, trashed, totaled. We're waiting; they're supposed to send a tow truck. She's good except she has to pee so she's—"

"Oh my God, did you just tell Jason that I have to pee? Now he's going to imagine me peeing. Don't forget to tell him we found the doll at a tag sale but we need to buy wrapping paper. At least we think it's the doll."

"You hear that? Yeah, don't think about her peeing. And we're pretty sure it's the right doll; we had to spend like three hours on Craigslist to find one."

Imagine that after the tow truck arrives and our couple has been safely installed into a rental vehicle, they don't really ever think about that crash again except both are pleased with the new car's color. Neither liked the wrecked Mercedes's particular shade of red.

In this example, you can see how your entire perception of what happened—and you were a witness—is completely distorted by your point of view.

So, if you were to enter therapy over being disturbed by

this wreck, you could spend years discussing why the sight of the doll was so upsetting, and how impotent you felt being unable to stop and help but even if you could stop, what could you have done?

Possibly, the therapist would have you write letters to the dead little girl.

What this really accomplishes is the creation of a sort of personal myth. A series of well-remembered events with finely honed details. As accurate as they may be, they are accurate from only one perspective.

For many years, I believed that one's past had to be fully understood in order to move through and beyond it. I see now that I was wrong about this. I know now that scrutinizing one's past and trying to gain understanding and "make peace" with it is a kind of addiction that keeps one focused on the past and not on the present.

As with any addiction, the first step to overcoming it is to see it.

And once you see it, you have to stop it.

II

Once the current moment moves into the past, it is entirely gone. It ceases to exist except in documents, photographs, and an impression left in a sofa cushion. The past—and all the moments it contained—are no longer sharing this world with us. They are no more real than Cinderella.

To spend time—year after year—in therapy or on your own thinking about your past and forming conclusions and stitching the elements into a narrative that you can name, "the truth," in order to be "free" of it, is not how you become free from your past.

The past does not need to be reconsidered in the present and given a structure. The events of the past cannot be understood when you are the only element of the past actively engaged in reliving it.

When somebody says, "Therapy has been really helpful to me in terms of resolving some of my issues from the past," what does this actually, in practical terms, mean?

Or somebody is "haunted" or controlled by their past. How is this possible?

When I first moved to New York, I became friends with a guy who seemed to be exactly the guy I wanted to be. He was very outgoing and had lots of friends and they probably all felt as I did: like his best and closest friend.

After we'd been friends for almost a year, one night we were out drinking and he told me he had a confession to make, something he wanted me to know about himself.

I nodded and tried to look very sincere and open, while inside my mind it was the Kentucky Derby, with most of the money being placed on female-to-male transsexual.

That wasn't it.

He proceeded to tell me in great detail about the utterly atrocious physical abuse he'd experienced at the hands of his father and mother during his childhood. It was well beyond anything I myself had ever come close to experiencing.

After this evening, my friend spoke of his past abuse frequently.

And I realized that all the time we'd been friends, all those moments prior to his revelation had probably been, in his mind, moments leading up to The Telling.

Only after The Telling could he be fully himself with me.

His story of his past abuse was a large part of his identity. It was a protected secret that was kept out of view for acquaintances and coworkers. Only after a measure of trust and intimacy had been formed would there be almost a ceremony in which he detailed his abuse. Rather like unwrapping, slowly, an extravagant gift one knows is going to blow the mind of the recipient.

When we first became friends it had amazed me that he was single. I now understood that he was single because of how guys reacted when my friend finally revealed his history. It was like encountering a new person. And my friend's abuse was now like a third person with us wherever we went.

Who could blame him? It was a wonder he was still alive.

Today, I see it differently.

My friend is a dramatic example of somebody who is haunted by their past. But because the past is gone, how does it haunt?

Of course, it does not. The past does not haunt us. We haunt the past. We allow our minds to focus in that direction. We open memories and examine them. We reexperience emotions we felt during the painful events we experienced because we are recalling them in as much detail as we can.

We enter therapy and discuss our past. We formulate opinions about what happened. We create a rich, detailed world. In therapy or on our own, we focus our attention on something that no longer exists in order to understand or have perspective or acknowledge or own what has happened. And only after we decide this understanding or recognition has taken place do we stop worrying that particular tooth with our tongue.

For years, I believed this was how to live.

I was wrong. It's how to stagnate.

I know now how to get over the past. It has worked for me in a deeper, more enduring way than any therapy I have ever had.

Writing six autobiographical books is what freed me from my past.

If the books had been cookbooks I expect I would feel just exactly as free. That I wrote six books about my past is the red herring; nothing I have written has in any way altered the past or healed me clean, so no scar remains.

Perhaps the process of writing—being fully in the moment, while I write letter by letter—has soothed me because it's kept me busy. When you're busy, you lack the time to fondle your emotional baggage. And if that sounds too reductive, remember we crawled from the swamp. Simple isn't such a terrible thing to be in this respect.

For the same reason, being out of a job and just hanging around is depressing in a thousand different ways. All you have is time. Sooner or later, you end up wandering around bad neighborhoods inside your head. Neighborhoods like, "They never should have fired me, those assholes." Which may be true or it may be untrue but it's irrelevant to everything.

It is through work that challenged me and required continuous freshness that I began to occupy not the past but this, right now. My advertising career had not been challenging. Being busy is not the same as being focused. Being focused means being *here*.

And this, *here,* this line, that comma.

That's what freed me from the past. The present kidnapped

me. I climbed into its car when it held up its hand and showed me the candy. I hopped right in.

When something from my past upsets me here in my present, it's because I let my mind think back to the past and grab hold of something.

This is how the past haunts us. We think about it.

Therapy could be of tremendous benefit to "getting over" one's past if the therapy is focused on specific ways to stop submitting to the temptation to obsess.

Many people with difficult histories carry these histories with them, burnishing the past with each retelling.

Consider this statement: "I was raped. It happened twenty years ago and even to this day, it still haunts me. I still find it very difficult to get on with my life."

Who could question such a statement?

Well, I could.

By suggesting if the following statement might be a more truthful statement. "I was raped. It happened twenty years ago. Many things in daily life remind me of the rape. Each time this happens, I allow myself to reflect on the moment I've been reminded of. And because my mind is occupied with my past, I am not focused on the present or the future."

When somebody experiences something truly horrific and shocking or so unimaginably painful and ruinous and they survive, all you can do is wonder, "But how?"

This is how: by living with what exists in our life right this moment. And by recognizing that the origin of what we have or do not have is irrelevant.

If you were raped twenty years ago and you suffered nerve damage that causes a partial paralysis in your leg when the temperature drops, what actually matters is, "What's the weather like today?" If it's cold, are you equipped to manage your paralysis?

It does not matter how you became paralyzed. It does not matter that you are paralyzed because your full functionality was taken from you.

The unfairness of your current status is unimportant.

What matters is, can you do what you need to do? If not, what can you do to achieve what you want to achieve?

It doesn't matter that you shouldn't have to be so fucking focused on the weather because he raped you and gave you nerve damage in your leg.

It matters that the temperature is going to cause you paralysis today and are you ready to manage it?

SOMETIMES, A PARTICULAR TRAUMA may be the largest thing we have ever experienced. So we kind of move into it, make it our home. Because there's nothing in our lives on the scale of that loss or that trauma.

So, you need a larger life. Something that can successfully compete with your past.

To live with your mind in the past—in the name of healing or understanding or overcoming—is to live in a fantasy world where nothing new or original is created. To "understand" one's past is to handle clay that no longer exists and shape it into a bowl nobody can ever see or touch.

Denial of the painful events in one's past is the same as obsessing over one's past. To actively refuse to discuss or think about, if need be, what happened is to imbue it with power.

Recycling the past into a new business, a not-for-profit to help others, a workshop, a painting, a book, a song—these are ways to explore the past in the context of the present. These are things people who are actively alive do.

You must never allow something that happened to you to become a morbidly treasured heirloom that you carry around, show people occasionally, put back in its black velvet pouch, and then tuck back into your jacket where you can keep it close to your heart.

Then, when asked to join the pole vaulting club, pull the coach aside and whisper, "I can't. See"—and remove your gem from your pocket—"this is my terrible thing and as I expected, showing it to you has taken your breath away and made you sympathetic. So I will be excused, I assume?"

Other people will allow you—they will never blame you or challenge you—to use your past as an excuse to not face the normal fears everybody has when facing their future.

Even if you were brutally physically assaulted, you must not withdraw because you are afraid it will happen again.

This is not a valid exit.

Your fears that it might happen again are perfectly reasonable and justified: it might happen again.

Many people believe that if something really bad happens to them, they have paid their dues and nothing else really bad can happen again. But on the day you attend your mother's funeral or declare personal bankruptcy, there is no law in the universe that prevents you from also getting a speeding ticket and your first grey hair.

When multiple bad things happen, it can feel like "life is out to get you." It's not. And it's not a sign, either.

What you do is, you keep going. You stop waiting for fairness.

III

You do not need to work through your past so you can heal. You need to move forward and then you're as healed as you're likely to be.

Unless.

Unless you experienced something so unspeakably terrible, something so out of scale in magnitude that it simply doesn't fit into the past. It is too large to be contained by time or space.

And if this is you, the thing you can do for the duration of your existence is to tell your story over and over. So that other people can hear you tell it and they can be moved, changed by it.

This can help others.

Which is the single comfort for people who will always remain locked in their history, inside something that is really a different species of awful.

I met somebody whose grandfather had survived the death camps in Germany.

He told me that his grandfather was a very quiet, broken man. He rarely spoke and when he did, he told the same stories about how he survived.

I told him, "Do you listen, every time he tells you?"

He said, "No, I just kind of let him talk and do my thing; I've heard it all a thousand times."

I wondered if he had ever truly heard it once. I suggested he listen, hang on every word and try to see visuals in his mind of the story his grandfather was telling him.

Some stories must be carved into the present and the future by telling and telling again and then again until the story is part of us.

How to Be a Good
Mental Patient

I F YOUR CAR WAS making a thunk, thunk, thunk sound
every time you hit the brakes and it was taking way too long
to come to a stop, you'd go to a mechanic. But you certainly
wouldn't waste time asking him to "Check out the glove com-
partment light and also the power seat on the passenger side.
And you know? Maybe you should also see if something might
be loose in the trunk."

But this is exactly what people frequently do when they see
a therapist to help them resolve personal issues.

I know many people who speak of therapy with a degree of
pride, as though being in therapy implies a state of superior
self-awareness or is a kind of *Good Housekeeping* seal of approval
for mental health. I was acquainted with one person who took
a measure of pride in pointing to a building and remarking, "I
think that's the building where my therapist and her husband
own a rental unit."

If you've become pals with your therapist, that's how you

know it's time to terminate the therapeutic relationship with this particular therapist.

Friendship pollutes objectivity.

Some therapists will disagree with this statement. These are precisely the therapists to avoid.

The best therapists are brilliantly insightful and gifted at pattern recognition. And they are not your buddy. Your advocate, yes. Your squash partner, no.

It's tricky because therapy is a business. So most therapists will encourage you to "make an investment" in the therapeutic process. In therapy, most issues take many months, if not years, to resolve.

In reality, I believe most issues can be resolved very quickly—as quickly as you can see the deeper truth of your situation.

One potential danger with entering into long-term therapy is that it's very easy to spend the time "revisiting" traumas of the past in order to "work through" them. Which to me is a graduate school way of saying "wallowing."

Revisiting painful experiences makes you experience the pain. When you need to move past something, this isn't helpful. What is helpful is realizing you don't need closure, you don't need understanding, and you don't need resolution. What difference would these things make if you had them?

Having one's mother or father or past abuser admit to their crimes or even apologize for them changes nothing—certainly not what they did. Rather, such an apology would give you the psychological permission to "move on" with your life.

But you do not need anybody's permission to move on with your life.

It does not matter whether or not those responsible for

harming you ever understand what they did, care about what they did, or apologize for it.

It does not matter.

All that matters is your ability to stop fondling the experience with your brain. Which you can do right now.

A good therapist can help by preventing you from spending time wallowing in the past and instead focus on organizing your future. A good therapist can also help you to think clearly when your head is too messy, which happens.

A therapist should be engaged with you and appear genuinely focused on what you are saying. They should be able to suggest connections they observe and offer concrete tools you can use to manage or solve your issues. If your therapist spends each session talking more than you do, especially if they are talking about their ideas or philosophies, this may be a sign of a therapist with some variety of messiah complex.

Likewise, your therapist should not be your audience. Your attempts to charm, humor, or otherwise ingratiate yourself to the therapist should fail. It is generally not helpful to have a therapist who thinks you're really funny and enjoys your company.

Try to see the therapist as more like a hooker.

People can relax and be honest around a hooker because they don't consider the hooker to be their equal. The hooker poses no threat and can offer no redemption. Any redemption you experience in the presence of a hooker—or a good therapist—is redemption you earned and were not given.

How to Make Yourself Uncomfortable (and Why You Should)

I

I STARTED SMOKING WHEN I was thirteen. But I didn't consider myself "a smoker" until I had been at it for almost twenty years.

By then, I had tried quitting several times and failed.

Why did nothing work?

I tried the gum, the patch, the pills, going cold turkey. I would last for a few days—once, I made it through a full month—but inevitably, something would happen, the stress would be too much, and there would be a pack of cigarettes in my pocket once again.

This is exactly what I said to a friend of mine in the late 1990s when he asked me why I was still smoking. All the other smokers we knew had quit.

As I explained how each method had failed, he nodded. "Oh, wow. I didn't realize you'd already tried everything."

I saw on his face that he did not hold me accountable for my not being able to quit any more than he would blame somebody whose chemo had failed. He said, "I wonder if nothing worked because you started when you were so young?"

I told him, "Yeah, I've wondered the same thing because I know two people who didn't start smoking until they were in college and when they quit, they just quit, boom. And when I tried doing that, it was totally impossible. So yeah, maybe if you start so young, that's it."

Then I saw with Windex clarity the truth: the patch didn't work, the gum didn't work, I've tried everything and everything has failed; and in the smug, small pleasure I took in saying that all these methods had failed me was my knowledge of, but refusal to admit, the truth that I alone had failed.

I bought time by pretending that it was up to the Method I chose to end my smoking for me. When one Method failed, I could continue to smoke, then try another—sliding all responsibility for my smoking and any health issues entirely away from me.

There was only one reason why I did this. It wasn't impossible to stop smoking, it wasn't painful or difficult. It was extremely simple, easier than smoking, in fact. No need to inconvenience my thumb by making it turn the wheel of a Bic lighter.

It was uncomfortable.

It was *only* uncomfortable.

And I didn't like being uncomfortable.

Feeling like you cannot stand one more minute doesn't mean you can't. You can, actually.

It's incredibly easy to stop smoking. And it's horrifically uncomfortable. Then not *quite* horrifically uncomfortable. Then it's damn uncomfortable. Then it's uncomfortable. Then it's not as uncomfortable as it was at first. Then it's not so bad. And then you don't smoke anymore. And you don't miss it.

II

Pain is interesting. I dislike it immensely but I've never experienced pain and boredom at the same time. Even when I had unending and severe pain in my lower back for several years I was never bored by the pain, though it exhausted me.

But discomfort seems to magnetically attract boredom and then act as a magnifying glass.

Pain can make you want to die. Discomfort can make you want to kill.

Chronic discomfort itself can be deadly.

III

When I was in rehab for alcoholism in April of 1995, one of the people I met spoke in a group therapy session about how this would be his fifth visit to a rehab hospital and it had to work this time.

As soon as he said that, I knew that "it" would not work.

And by "knowing" this, the implication was that for me, it would.

I don't know whether this person remained sober but I relapsed and almost died. I had stayed sober for a year and a half, then started drinking when a friend began to die.

I had paid such careful attention to the relapse prevention, learning about the triggers that can cause a person to drink, understanding how I could expect to feel after one month, two, six, nine.

I wrote and spoke frequently about my alcoholism and my cravings for the same reason people sometimes make noise when they walk through the woods: to let the predators know you are there; to keep them away.

As was suggested, I had visualized my "addict" as separate from me, a willful and destructive madman who wanted only to trick me and then bring me back to the bottle. I saw relapse as a dark figure that lurked in the unexamined corners of my life.

The powerlessness that is part of twelve-step recovery programs made me feel, I imagine, like a woman must feel when she is walking through a parking lot at night by herself.

Relapse had become a noun, not a verb.

So when I bought the alcohol and took it home with me and then sat at my computer, unscrewed the bottle, and began to drink, I was genuinely surprised that I never once lost control.

I saw then, I had prepared myself for something that did not exist. And failed to prepare myself for something that did: the possibility that I would ever again just decide, I'm going to drink.

It was as effortless as deciding on the spur of the moment to buy a pack of gum.

IV

When I stopped the next time, it would be two years later and life or death. I would face this choice and decide, death.

Then, change my mind.

The way I stopped drinking this time was by not purchasing or consuming alcohol. And that's all. Since I stopped drinking thirteen years ago, I've not had one craving for a drink. I've bought bottles of wine for others as gifts, but even when holding one of these bottles, not only have I not experienced the temptation to drink, but at the time I lacked even awareness of the missing temptation. I felt more like somebody who had never had an interest in drinking than somebody who very nearly drank himself out of existence.

I did not attend AA or see a therapist. I didn't keep track of how many days had passed since my last drink, as I did the first time. And I did not plan or even consider that this "not drinking" would evolve naturally into so many years of sobriety.

The difference in my mind the last time I stopped drinking is that I decided I was going to spend my life writing.

Later, I engaged with the activity that preceded writing for me: photography. But my sobriety never wavered.

The change in my mind was this: the first time I stopped drinking, I was ambitious and wanted to get sober, then be sober.

The last time I stopped drinking, I needed to write. And then, I needed to build a life with the person I had met. I needed dogs.

I didn't consider the quality of my "sobriety" this time, as I had before. I never felt the need to even wonder if I would ever drink again.

How to Finish Your Drink

I HAVE COME TO believe several things about how to quit drinking. One is that AA was very interesting and helpful to me when I attended meetings in 1995 because it was comforting to see other alcoholics and to see how people who were so different could come together and express feelings and experiences that were so intimately similar.

But I don't believe AA was useful in achieving or maintaining sobriety. It was interesting and comforting, but not of any particular use.

It's important to understand what AA actually is. It's not a company or an organization with a structure like the Salvation Army or Weight Watchers. It's really composed of individuals who agree to meet at a certain place and at a certain time to listen to members discuss their experiences as drinkers and detail the problems alcohol has caused in their lives. Considering the lack of any staff or even chain of command, the meetings are remarkably similar and structured. Multibillion-dollar retail chains suffer less consistency.

But woven into the philosophy of AA are certain concepts that I feel undermine sobriety. The first is the requirement that one admit to powerlessness over alcohol. And probably, this is—along with the spiritual "higher power" aspect—one of the more frequent struggling points for those new to AA.

My problem with admitting to powerlessness over alcoholism is that it isn't true. It was always a choice, though in the very late stage of my alcoholism, I made the choice by rote, never even considering the option not to drink. By then, it was extremely uncomfortable to be sober. Physically and mentally horribly uncomfortable.

I actually think one must assume power in order to be sober. One must not give oneself the permission to drink or relapse that the powerlessness of being alcohol's victim provides.

Another feature of AA is its slogans. Some, like "What you focus on grows," are profound to a cosmological degree.

Others, however, I believe encourage drinking. "Progress, not perfection" and "relapse is part of recovery" are two such slogans.

AA is based on submission and humility and for this reason, alcoholics keep count of the number of days, then weeks, then months, then years, they have maintained their sobriety. As with all things in which there is a score, these numbers evolve meaning. Reaching a certain number is rewarded with a token; relapsing results in forfeiting all of one's accumulated days and starting the count from zero again.

What I don't like about this is that the score keeping introduces an unnecessary and potentially dangerous element of *currency* into sobriety.

In a program based on printed text—twelve steps, printed onto posters and hung on every wall of every AA meeting worldwide—and slogans, known to most members and frequently utilized in meetings, a statement such as, "relapse is part of recovery" becomes something close to an instruction. But if falling short of this, it certainly implies that a lack of relapse would be out of the ordinary.

So in a way, one exists within AA knowing they will at some point drink again because to not drink would be "perfection" and to drink would be a "relapse" and "part of recovery." The price paid would be the number of days one was willing to lose.

All of this is a great deal of time spent in the company of alcohol, even if one isn't consuming the stuff. Drinking alcohol with your mind isn't freedom.

Talking about alcohol every day when you can't drink isn't going to work for everyone.

For this reason, AA strikes me not as the cure for alcoholism, but as the next best thing to drinking and the place to bide your time safely and without judgment until you do.

What has worked for me is to find something I wanted *more* than I wanted to drink, which was a fuck of a lot.

This is less a decision than a discovery. And it's for this reason that not everybody will get sober.

My view that the way to stop drinking is to stop drinking is laughably simplistic on the surface. It's "Just say no."

It's also true. The way to stop drinking is to want sobriety more. And then when you feel a craving, feel the craving until it passes. But don't act on it—any more than you wouldn't kill somebody you feel like killing when they cut you off in traffic.

Just because you want something doesn't mean you have to have it.

I know how infuriating that is to hear.

Relapse is the temper tantrum you allow yourself to have when you forbid yourself from drinking.

To stop drinking, you stop drinking. You pour it out right now.

Everything else—all the books, therapies, and programs—are merely hand-holding. They all strike to accomplish the same thing: to talk you into not drinking.

I'm saying, if you want to stop, you will. But most do not want to stop enough to actually stop. And until there's a medical fix, alcoholics will die as drunks.

To be successful at not drinking, a person needs to occupy the space in life drinking once filled with something more rewarding than the comfort and escape of alcohol. This is the thing you have to find.

You might not. Most alcoholics won't.

The truth is that people who cannot stop drinking are people who, however guilty they may feel and however dire the consequences, have become so addicted to the drug and the experience that they prefer it to the remainder of their lives. While they may truly want to be sober, they want to drink more.

The thought that precedes a relapse—certainly in my case and I bet in others as well—is, "screw it." Screw it is an idiom that means, "I no longer care."

Taking a drink is the opposite of powerlessness. It is taking firm, decisive action to terminate a state of sobriety that feels less satisfying and less convincing than drinking has felt in the past or we imagine will feel in the present. It may feel like one is powerless because it's frustrating to be unable to authentically want the thing you really want to want. But don't.

As a drug, alcohol is cunning. Because most alcoholics do have a measure of control over their drinking, often for many years. This changes, when it does, suddenly and profoundly. In late-stage alcoholism, the physical effects from abstinence are not only painfully uncomfortable but they can be fatal. At this stage, the alcoholic requires alcohol.

AA advertises a majority success rate. The advertisement is in the form of one of AA's foundation documents. "Rarely have we seen a person fail who has thoroughly followed our path." The implied efficacy brings to mind the question of, "Who's 'we'?"

The twelve-step program is frequently the first and primary course of treatment administered for a diagnosis of alcoholism, which is medically classified as a disease. I can think of no other standard medical treatment that is supported by little or no research and offers patients no statistical information regarding efficacy.

Still, many people swear by AA and have maintained lengthy periods of sobriety within it. For these people, the spiritual foundation and community of AA provide something that is, on the whole, more satisfying for them than drinking.

I don't believe that AA has "kept" these people sober. They have, instead, found something that has enabled them to choose a life without drinking. Many members of AA credit the program with keeping them sober; but they themselves are the reason.

The myth that alcoholics are powerless and unable in any way to shape the outcome of their addiction is a fatal, deeply untruthful message. No alcoholic should ever feel powerless over alcohol.

Those who die were not powerless. They either chose alcohol or they slid passively into the inevitable outcome of drinking; they made a decision by choosing to take no new action. And it's this choice that results in death.

That there exists a medically recognized *disease* that is typically treated through twelve-step programs that are based on vague supernatural components is shocking to me. If breast cancer or leukemia were treated in such a medieval fashion, there would be riots.

Ultimately, the treatment for addiction—until and if there is a successful medication—resides within the addict. You can't spend time waiting for rehab to "work" or for something to "fix" you. These things can—and do—inspire you or encourage you.

You don't need to take action to stop drinking. Drinking is an action: pouring the vodka into the glass, raising the glass to your lips.

To stop drinking, all you have to do is sit.

In 100 percent of the documented cases of alcoholism worldwide, the people who recovered all shared one thing in common, no matter how they did it:

They didn't do it.

They just didn't do it.

You absolutely can stop drinking today, right now.

The question is only, do you want to be sober more than you want to drink?

Very few people can answer this question truthfully and reply, yes.

I hope you're one of them. Maybe you are.

I didn't think I was.

How to Hold on to Your Dream or Maybe Not

I

EVERY TIME I WATCH some trembling, weepy girl stand at the podium to accept her best female pop vocal performance Grammy and start thanking her ICM agent and God, I cringe because I know what's next. "And I just want to say to every little girl watching out there tonight, listen to me: never, never give up your dream. If your dream is to stand here where I am, you don't let anybody stop you. And I promise, someday the world will be watching *you* up here."

I just want to ask one of these singers, have you ever watched a single one of the many thousands of abysmal covers of your own song that are on YouTube? Because those are dreams. Dreams are not always beautiful things.

I know these Grammy winners in their spaghetti strap gowns mean well but there are many, many people who do not need to be told to cling to their dreams; they need to have those dreams wrenched from their little fists before they waste their entire lives trying to achieve them.

I am one such person.

IT FELT LIKE A physical touch, a thumb firmly but gently pressing along the path of my sternum.

I just knew.

You know?

My certainty was that thumb pressing my chest. As I stood in front of the other students in the acting class, in Amherst, Massachusetts, in 1981. And while they watched me, I looked over their seated heads at the wall, yet in a way watched myself.

And by watched myself, I mean, I really saw myself.

I may have held just the slightest British accent in my voice because I loved movies from the forties, especially the way the actors said our ordinary American words with English-flavored flair.

"Half as big as life, that's me," I said. And as I said it, it was as if my eyes were two windows facing a gray, endless pelt of rain. "Half as big as life, that's small. But deep in my heart I can feel that I'm ten feet tall. Ten feet tall."

That rhyme—along with several others, throughout the monologue—had itched me initially because there was something so *cute* about it. Kind of cloyingly cute. Not my thing, really. It seemed chirpy. But I ignored this concern and memorized it anyway, because this was easier than selecting another play; one without rhyming dialogue.

I told myself, this is an incredible opportunity. To take this dusty, forgotten play yanked from its grave of a shelf and make it amazing. That would be a real accomplishment.

The more I read, the more I loathed the play. This struck me as right. I had always needed to defy the odds, hadn't I? I had always needed to be the one who finds a diamond ring, right there in a mound of old dog poop.

I would take what was obviously a play written not by a writer but by a happy person who was given a typewriter for Christmas and I would turn it into a dramatic masterpiece.

Which is exactly what I did in class the following week.

As I stood before the other students delivering my mono-logue with chilling emotional precision, I could actually *feel* how good I was. Goosebumps rose on my arms and, surely, on the arms of the other students and the teacher as well.

I was going to be one of the—or possibly *the*—greatest ac-tors of my day. I had known since a very young age that I con-tained extra colors within my emotional range that I did not see displayed in other people but that they recognized when they saw these colors in me.

That's the only way I can describe my certainty that I was born to act, to inhabit other people. Because I, my own self, could not make connections with others. And when I did, they were staged. I had always been acutely self-conscious, as though I spoke a separate, small, little-known language and didn't want to give myself away.

My inability to touch other people now made perfect sense.

And as I finished my monologue, I felt the first calm I had ever known. As though I had been handed a gilded-paged vol-ume called *Life*. And I had been allowed to open the book and look up the answer to the question of me.

What happened next remains so vivid that even in private, my face flushes.

The acting teacher looked at me with an expression like,

"This can't be true, but this is true, right?" and she asked, "You know, that's not a monologue. Right? I'm curious to know why you chose to use the lyrics of a song from *Promises, Promises* as your piece? Maybe it's an interesting concept to explore, but have a seat and let me play it back for you."

Thank the Lord Jesus for making video recorders and playback decks at just exactly the right moment in time. Because I was able to now see myself not in my own mind, but rather with my own eyes.

And it was a stunning revelation.

The *knowledge* that I was giving an incredible performance in no way aligned with the reality of what I saw before me. Except for the nervous twitch of my left eyelid, the motionless figure on the screen appeared to be a JCPenney mannequin.

At first, I actually thought something might be wrong with the machine. But I thought this only for the briefest instant.

Because I then had another physical sensation: one of falling—but not far—and landing—but not hard—at the bottom of something dark with an earthy, repulsive, yet comforting floor. I felt myself land on the very bottom, the flesh of the earth, the ground everything in the world is built on top of and hides from view.

I fell and landed on the truth.

Not the truth I believed in my heart or the truth I wanted to be true, but the truth in a more mathematical sense. Like, "Yes or no: you are wearing shoes at this moment?"

That is what truth is. Truth is an unassailable fact. Not your opinion of the fact. Nor is the truth your report of the events from your own, uniquely distorted and biased view, where there could be a disco ball hanging in the way blocking the most important element.

Which, in this case, happened to be the fact, the truth that I sucked worse than anything has ever sucked in the history of suckage, at acting.

I did not have the expressive range required to deliver the title of the monologue, let alone the meaning contained within the words.

What I felt, what I saw myself express, the nuance, the authenticity, existed entirely inside my bright red head.

I saw this for myself and I recognized immediately, this is not the kind of thing where improvement is possible.

If you bake a cake and the cake sinks in the middle, you can hop in the car and drive over to Quik Mart, pick up another can of vanilla-flavored frosting, and then load up the sunken center with that whole can and when you bring it to the table, it will look spectacular. There: you improved the fallen cake. Until, of course, somebody actually bites into it and their teeth get a razor stubble burn from the sugar, but at least until that happens, improvement has occurred.

But you cannot do this if the cake has baked itself out of the pan and gone missing.

Nothing does not get better with hard work and dedication.

I was not an actor.

Okay.

What now?

It took a long time, but I became a writer. Which is the same thing, except I'm better at it. Probably because I can be alone when I do it.

I have absolutely no regret.

When I ask myself, why did I want to be an actor?

The answer is so plain: to be with people, to reach them.

In my normal life, this is very, very difficult for me.

But writing has allowed me to reach people and feel a connection.

I don't feel I gave up my dream. I gave up my choice of vehicle used to deliver me to this dream.

I thought it would be a big-ass Ford pickup and instead it was a pale blue hatchback.

The worst advice we're given on the subject of dreams happens each year during the Academy Awards.

Sooner or later, the best sound editor, composer of an original score, or supporting actress will stare directly into the camera, not the audience, but right at us—the person at home in the dark watching—and say, "I am the proof. Never, never give up your dream."

When you hear those words spoken by a total winner, and backed with so much obviously sincere emotion, it resonates inside you and you think, "Oh my God, she is totally right. I was about to give up hope. But I won't. I'm going to keep at it."

When in truth, if you happen to lack talent at whatever it is you want in life, and if you never stop trying to attain it, you will spend your life feeling like a movie with an out-of-sync soundtrack.

What you have to do is know the truth.

The problem is that nobody else can tell you. Only you know what you contain. What others see of you is only what you show them.

All of us are richer and more fascinating and more complex than we can ever know.

If you want to be a singer and maybe you just are so annoyed by your stupid brother and irritating parents you never, not once, sang anything in their presence aside from a begrudging

"Happy Birthday" now and then, but you have spent years singing privately, maybe recording yourself and you're 99 percent
certain you're not just fooling yourself, then I agree with the
winner for the best sound design in a foreign film under four
and a half minutes: never give up your dream. Or if you can't
really sing all that well and you are gifted with both the ability
to realistically and objectively appraise your own talent but also
supplement it with showmanship or "star quality," then I also
feel you should cling to this dream and make it happen.

It's a little confusing because in some cases, the right thing
to do is to hold on to your dream, even if maybe you're not the
best at whatever it is. The key is self-knowledge. If you *know*
you were meant to be a rock star and you realize this defies
reason to some extent but still, your certainty does not waver
and there is no other possible life for you, you must pursue
your dream. Probably. Even though it's actually quite rare to
become hugely successful at something you're not all that great
at, just because you are so skilled at compensating in other areas. It's rare because there are so many other people who want
the same thing and are actually quite excellent. What's also
rare is the self-possession to continue in pursuit of one's dream
in spite of this knowledge.

And *rare* is valuable.

If you feel almost the same except you can imagine another
kind of life, like being a vet tech, and you wonder if this is
what you should do, that "wondering" could be the weak link.

Another way to think about it is like this: if you *can* let go
of the dream, you probably should.

If you can't let go of the dream, don't.

People who live with regret over not "following their
dreams" are frequently people who did actually have the talent

or the charisma or the whatever-it-takes to have found success and they can see this now; they wish they had just followed their instincts *back then*.

People who did follow their dreams but never found the success they expected, walk away with the door prize of being that person who followed their dreams, no matter what.

That's a lot harder than just entering medical school and coming out the other end a doctor.

When one's dreams and one's abilities are aligned, it is faith and dedication that are most required.

Where there is a distinct misalignment between the dream and the talent, before deciding to pursue the dream anyway, you must test its seaworthiness.

You must examine this dream of yours.

The question to ask yourself is, why?

Why do you want to be a pharmacist? Why, if you cannot have biological children and not used, adopted ones, is your life not worth living?

You need to grab your dream out of the sky like it's a kite and pinch the string through your fingers until you reach the spool.

When you taste or smell or feel this dream of yours, how would you describe that residue?

If you immediately imagine yourself on a private jet surrounded by bodyguards and wearing eighteen-carat diamond-drop earrings, you're in luck. That's an easy one. You don't want to be a singer; you want to be hugely wealthy. So you need to invent something the world wants. Like a conveyer belt runway for jets, so small countries like Japan can increase their landing and takeoff capacity while reducing the amount of acreage spent.

Or become a supersuccessful criminal. Or write a stupidly amazing Facebook game.

Dreams often have a misty, smeared, watercolor resolution. So we don't always try to rack them into focus and ask, "Okay, why do I want this?"

You have to do this. The rock-bottom, earthy truth is exactly the only thing that can make you happy and satisfied in your life.

I blame kindergarten.

That's where we're all taught that everybody is "equal" and can "do anything!" When in fact, we are as equal as squids and puppies.

In the last century I dated an Italian who, like most Long Island–bred Italians, continued to do his laundry at home, despite the fact that he occupied a one-bedroom apartment in Midtown with its own built-in washer and dryer. But it was the frequency with which he called his mother on the phone that made me feel like I was involved in an interspecies relationship.

The Italian Who Basically Still Lives at Home had a teenage sister. He'd spoken of her frequently. The whole family believed she might well be the next Meryl Streep, right there in their midst, hogging the bathroom.

When I finally met his family, I was both puzzled and disturbed. His sister was very open and genuinely warm with lots of kinky red hair. She was mentally disabled by some degree of retardation. It made the girl anxious to operate a fork because she didn't want to screw up and spill something. I could see it on her face and it made me ache with tenderness for her. It made me think if I had such a child who was afraid to use her fork for fear of dropping it, I would be the bad parent that says, "screw forks," and the family would always eat with their hands like cave people. I don't care if that's fucked up; I know I'd do it anyway. Unless I could make her laugh by eating with a straw, then that's what we'd do. For the rest of our lives.

The girl's family all spoke of her as though she was an honors student at Juilliard. While she sat right in front of them at the dinner table, struggling with her noodles.

"Believe me, you: I know talent. And that girl's got it," Vincent's mother said.

Vincent's father was the only one who even came close to admitting the truth about the girl; he said nothing and kept himself mostly tucked into his plate.

After the plates had been cleared, the girl abruptly stood and shrieked, "You know how whistle, Stee. You puh the libs together in the blow."

The family members clapped vigorously.

The girl said the line once again.

In their combined denial and attempt to bolster the girl's confidence, they had *misinformed* her.

Then she turned to me and said, "I have Oscar and he made of gold? And I will win him. And mirror street will not get to have him because I get to."

"She means 'Meryl Streep,'" the mother told me. "She's saying she's going to win the Oscar and not *Meryl Streep*. I'll tell you one thing, that girl is no small dreamer."

THAT EVENING WHEN WE returned to The Italian's apartment, I gently broached the subject. "So . . . what's the deal with your family and Mel? It's like nobody seems to even know what's up with her."

He pried one shoe off his heel using the toe of the other. "What do you mean, what's up with her?"

"Well, it's great that everybody is so encouraging around her and she's nuts about you, but, what I mean is, because she's obviously mentally retarded to some degree, is there a risk she might take this encouragement literally? And, like, in real life want to be a movie star?"

Which is when I learned that the only thing that you can say to an Italian that's worse than "Your mother charges twenty dollars extra if you want her to swallow" is "your sister is mentally retarded," even if it's completely true.

He didn't punch me. Instead, he turned around and he opened the door and stood back. He didn't say a word but he motioned with his head, *out*.

It would be five years before we spoke again. He called to tell me I had been right, his sister was mentally impaired. They had learned this when she began to go on auditions in the city and she had been confused.

She was happy now, though. She was almost eighteen and was working at a company that made biodegradable soy-based packing material. Her job was to count things, then click, then do this again and again until it was time to go home. He said she loved it.

SOMETIMES IT'S NOT QUITE so obvious that the dream is the wrong size, color, and shape for the dreamer. That's when encouraging somebody to keep their dream alive borders on cruel.

No. There's no bordering. It is cruel. It's just accidentally, well-intentioned cruelty.

It is not true that you can do anything you set your mind to.

It is a lie that with hard work and perseverance, you can achieve your dream.

And it's better for you to know this: wanting something with all your heart does not mean you're good enough at it.

Letting go of a dream because it cannot be yours is not failing. There are many ways to fail in life but this is not among them.

The other thing about dreams you must know is that they are not like spleens. There is not just one per person.

And here's the hardest truth: you are the only person to judge whether or not you do have the talent or skill or ability to make your dream come true or you don't. Nobody else can tell you because you may be holding in reserve something extra, something more and rare, and very much enough. Only you know.

II

We think of dreams as belonging only to the young, like smooth skin or mononucleosis. Yet dreams may not only *last* a lifetime—sometimes you must wait almost a lifetime to see them come true.

Most people know the story of Grandma Moses, the American painter who achieved worldwide fame when she was "a grandma." It's become a cliche to invoke her name when talking about how dreams can come true at any age.

But most people are not aware of the specifics.

When her husband of forty years died, Grandma Moses was almost seventy herself. She took up needlepoint. But by the time she was seventy-six, the arthritis in her hands forced her to give it up.

So she decided she'd paint.

She was nearly eighty when her work was exhibited at New York's Museum of Modern Art.

Which made her famous.

For the rest of her life she painted and traveled around the world showing her work in galleries, appearing on magazine covers, and being an art world celebrity.

This went on for the next twenty years. So it's not like she achieved her dream at an old age, then dropped over dead. Her career as a painter lasted longer than Van Gogh's.

And it didn't even begin until she was almost twice as old as he was when he died.

How to Identify Love by Knowing What It's Not

L OVE DOESN'T USE A fist.
Love never calls you fat or lazy or ugly.

Love doesn't laugh at you in front of friends.

It is not in Love's interest for your self-esteem to be low.

Love is a helium-based emotion; Love always takes the high road.

Love does not make you beg.

Love does not make you deposit your paycheck into its bank account.

Love certainly never, never, never brings the children into it.

Love does not ask or even want you to change. But if you change, Love is as excited about this change as you are, if not more so. And if you go back to the way you were before you changed, Love will go back with you.

Love does not maintain a list of your flaws and weaknesses.

Love believes you.

Love is patient; Love does not make a point of showing you how patient it is. It is critical to understand the distinction.

Patience is like donating a large sum of money to a charity anonymously. What matters to you as the donor is that the charity receives the funding, not who wrote the check, even if knowing who donated such a huge check would wildly impress the world.

So, patience is exhibited only by a lack of pressure. This is how you know it's there.

But when you see on the face of your partner or spouse an expression that reads, "I'm being very patient with you," this could be the single detail that alerts you to the fact that you are in an abusive relationship.

You can be in such a relationship and not even know it. You can receive so many black eyes, you forgot it's abnormal to have even one.

Physical violence is one kind of abuse. Emotional violence is another kind of abuse. These assaults are delivered with concepts. People usually say, emotional abuse is about words: fat, ugly, stupid, lazy. But it's not about words because an emotionally abusive person doesn't always resort to using the verbal club, but rather the verbal untraceable poison.

They may, in fact, speak very kind words to you. And appear nothing but supportive to those around you. Their covert abuse is administered in small, cunning ways. Over time. So the impact is gradual, not fist-to-the-eye immediate.

An abusive partner is controlling. They are manipulative. They might make a special point of coyly sharing information that they actually know will upset you. They might supply reasonable arguments as to why they and not you should make important decisions.

If you possess talent or a natural ease and comfort with a particular ability and your abusive partner is resentful, abuse might arrive in the form of subtraction: no remark at all, not a compliment or a gesture of support. Perhaps one small, internally flawless diamond of a criticism will be presented.

Silence when there should be discussion to resolve an issue is another method of abuse if the silence is used as a tool to frustrate or sadden or otherwise intentionally manipulate the emotions of another.

I knew of somebody—part of the same couple I mentioned earlier—who was many years into an abusive relationship but did not know it. She knew only that she had been so happy when they met and that it seemed to her this feeling was bled out of her year after year, and she found that she now resembled her partner, whom she had once seen as strong and silent and loving but had come to understand was emotionally disturbed and was not silent in his mind, but roiling.

When she finally left him she did so still loving him. She had been more financially stable so she had given him their home. He had admitted to her that for the last couple of years, he had been occupied with planning his suicide. He told her he'd worked out all the details and would do it in a quaint West Coast town right on the Pacific that they had frequently spoke of visiting but never seen.

When she left him she left their beloved dog with him because she worried a totally empty house would be dangerous.

Their plan had been to share the dog but he wanted nothing more to do with her. And the regular updates and photographs he had sent when they first parted stopped now completely.

Months passed and she heard nothing until he sent a brief

email informing her that the dog now had a potential serious health problem and that he would take care of it.

She could not help but feel that he had taken a small measure of satisfaction knowing how brutal the news would be to her ears and how helpless she would feel being able to do nothing, not even see this dog she had loved for so long.

Emotional abuse is the process of breaking the spirit or shattering the confidence of another for one's own purpose.

Abusive people never change. There is no point of pursuing couples' therapy when one member of the relationship is abusive. A therapist may tell you otherwise. But I'm telling you the not-for-profit truth. Abusers do not change.

It will only get worse.

The difference between physical violence like a slap on the face or a shove and homicide can be as small as a few centimeters or the angle of approach.

Also, abusers are always very, very sorry. Men who abuse women probably shed more tears in one year than the combined tears of all the girls in the audience of a Renée Zellweger movie opening weekend at the Paris Theatre in Manhattan.

That's how sorry he is.

Or so he says, with his tears.

Of course, he's not sorry. She is.

Unless the roles are reversed. And the abuser is a woman, not a man.

Women can and do physically and emotionally abuse their partners. The perception that the abuser is always a man is false.

One need only live near a lesbian bar like I did in the mid-nineties to know what sons of bitches women can be. Especially if they're shit-faced and pumped up on early Indigo Girls.

People remain in abusive relationships for the same reasons they remain in loving ones: they've built a life together, they have children, financial interests, habit, nothing better. Lots of reasons.

But probably the number-one reason is simply not knowing they're in one.

You think of domestic violence and you think of a character and a weak victim: macho, powerful bully and a passive, frail woman and you don't recognize that. So it can't be you.

It might help, then, for me to show you in clinical terms what domestic violence actually looks like on the printed page. This checklist is from the National Domestic Violence Hotline. Ask yourself, does your partner:

- Embarrass you with put-downs
- Look at you or act in ways that scare you
- Control what you do, who you see or talk to, or where you go
- Stop you from seeing your friends or family members
- Take your money or Social Security check, make you ask for money, or refuse to give you money
- Make all of the decisions
- Tell you that you're a bad parent or threaten to take away or hurt your children
- Prevent you from working or attending school
- Act like the abuse is no big deal, it's your fault, or even deny doing it
- Destroy your property or threaten to kill your pets
- Intimidate you with guns, knives, or other weapons

- Shove you, slap you, choke you, or hit you
- Force you to try and drop charges
- Threaten to commit suicide
- Threaten to kill you

Think about the answers before you answer. Does he prevent you from working? No, he encourages you, that's terrific.

Or does he?

Does he *maybe* prevent you a little by getting drunk and then, say, being unable to find a certain pair of shoes so he turns the house upside down, creating such a scene, a ME, ME, ME moment that you can't possibly work?

Might he always, over and over, bring it all back to himself? Leaving no room or time for you to work on your crafts, aka possible future home business aka threat to him?

Domestic violence is extremely difficult to detect when it is happening to you because domestic violence always only happens to other people, and you are too smart and sophisticated to ever, for one moment, be with somebody abusive. The thought is absurd. Domestic violence is a lower-class problem, something that afflicts only those whose homes are clad in aluminum siding.

Besides, you would know if you were being abused.

Except the truth is, some things are too terrible to know; too impossible to see; too painful to realize; too heartbreaking to face.

You could be in an abusive relationship and be unaware that you are, unable to see the abuse for what it is.

Sometimes the truth must unspool slowly. It's simply

impossible to grasp it all at once. Perhaps, one day, you will be able to see a glimpse of abuse in your relationship.

In time, you'll be able to see more.

Because if you allow yourself to have one small serving of reality, the hard part, the opaque part, is over. And eventually, you'll be able to see the rest.

Also, the more unlikely it is that you would ever be in an abusive relationship, the closer you need to look at your relationship. Not because you want to try to see something sinister that simply isn't there, but because you're more likely to be blind to abuse if it is there.

Just, you know, pay attention. To all those familiar, everyday things they say to you or do to you. Ask, "If he said that to my friend, would I think it was mean?"

Try to actually hear what the person says to you. Try to hear it fresh. Try to see if what they say to you might, in a way, also be a kind of steering wheel.

It's a spectrum, too. Maybe your partner isn't exactly "abusive" so much as a little controlling. This is fairly easy to see.

What's difficult to see is when you're with somebody who is a full-strength abuser. And maybe one reason it's so difficult to see something that to the rest of the world—at least on paper—is so obvious is because there's no contrast. They are controlling and abusive and this is what they are.

If you realize you are in an abusive relationship, you may want to call this phone number—it's toll-free so it won't cost you anything and it won't show up on your phone bill. If possible, take the number with you and call from somewhere else:

National Domestic Violence Hotline 1-800-799-SAFE (7233)

Seventy-nine-nine, seventy-two, thirty-three.

If you have children and your spouse is abusing them physically, mentally, or sexually, leave now.

It never takes courage to leave.

It takes love.

How to Live Unhappily Ever After

I JUST WANT TO be happy."

I can't think of another phrase capable of causing more misery and permanent unhappiness. With the possible exception of, "Honey, I'm in love with your youngest sister and she's agreed to marry me so I'd like a divorce."

Yet at first glance, it seems so guileless. Children just want to be happy. So do puppies and some middle-aged custodians.

Happy seems like a healthy, normal desire. Like wanting to breathe fresh air or shop only at Whole Foods.

But "I just want to be happy" is a hole cut out of the floor and covered with a rug.

Here's the problem: when you say to yourself or somebody else, "I just want to be happy," the implication is that you're not.

So what you want is something you don't have.

That's a mole behind your ear. Maybe it's just a mole and that's all it is. Wanting health insurance when you don't have it, wanting your kids to get a good education—nothing troubling about that.

But maybe that mole is something worse that's going to spread. And you become a person who moves frantically through life grabbing things off the shelf—the dark-haired boyfriend with the great parents since the blond musicians haven't worked out so well, the breast implants because then you'll like your body, the law degree that will make your father so proud of you and maybe you'll learn to like the law—but never managing to find the right thing, the one thing that will finally make you feel you aren't missing something essential, such as the point.

The "I just want to be happy" bear trap is that until you define precisely, just exactly what "happy" is, you will never feel it.

By defining what "happy" means to you in absolutely concrete terms you can then see what actions you need to take—or subtractions you need to make—to be able to say, "Yup, okay. This is the happy I was looking for. I've got it now. It's safe to get the breast implants."

If you're not a bespoke sort of person, you could use the standard, off-the-shelf definition.

Happiness is "a state of well-being characterized by emotions ranging from contentment to intense joy."

It's probably far-fetched to think you could be in a state of intense joy for most of the day. But maybe you could be mostly content.

Whatever being happy means to you, it needs to be specific and also possible. Maybe if you didn't have to go to work every day at a job you only tolerate but instead started your own online jewelry business. Maybe this would make you happy because you love jewelry; you find it interesting, you like to make it, you like the people who like it.

When you have a blueprint for what happiness is, lay it over your life and see what you need to change so the images are more aligned.

This recipe of defining what happiness means to you and then fiddling with your life to make the changes needed to make yourself happy will work for some people. But not for others.

I am one of the others.

I am not a happy person.

There are things that do make me experience joy. But joy is a fleeting emotion, like a very long sneeze.

I feel contentment rarely, but I do feel it.

A lot of the time what I feel is interested. Or I feel melancholy. And I also frequently feel tenderness, annoyance, confusion, fear, hopelessness, friskiness.

It doesn't all add up to anything I would call happiness.

What I'm thinking is, is that so terrible?

I used to say "I just want to be happy" all the time. I said it so frequently and without care that I forgot to refill the phrase with meaning, so it was just a shell of words.

When I said these words, I had only a vague sense of what happiness even meant to me.

I can see it in others. I even know one person who is happy 95 percent of the time, seriously. He's not stupid. As a matter of fact, he's right here beside me as I write, his own computer on his own lap organizing his playlist. And he makes me happy more often than I have ever been happy. But I will never be as happy as he is. And I don't mind this because I might not appreciate his happiness so much if I had it, too.

Also, I know a physicist who loves his work. People mistake his constant focus and thought with unhappiness. But he's not unhappy. He's busy. I bet when he dies, there will be a book on his chest.

Happiness is a wonderful goal for those who are inclined on a genetic level toward that emotional end of the spectrum.

Happiness is a treadmill of a goal for people who are not happy by nature.

Being an unhappy person does not mean you must be sad or dark. You can be interested instead of happy. You can be fascinated instead of happy.

How to Feel Less Regret

R EGRET IS A HOLLOW thing.
Regret is the lost and found of life. You can go there and sit and be one half of something that belongs to something else that isn't there anymore. You can wait and wait and wait and wish that everything, all of it, had turned out a different way. But wishing is the meal you only dreamed you ate. In regret, you still remain so fully half, and entirely unclaimed.

Regret is the feeling at the very bottom of impossible.

Regret is like a diamond: it's forever. Once you have entered a state of regret, you do not leave it.

It is not overbearing, like grief. Unlike grief, it does not transform into something else or get less intense over time.

Like all the other high-octane feelings—anger, jealousy, love—regret can be burned as fuel. In fact, it should be. Regret should power something beneficial.

To live in regret and change nothing else in your life is to miss the entire point.

Each thing should change you, if ever so slightly.

You can use regret to fuel learning so you do not repeat mistakes. You can use it to fuel art so that you spend a great deal of time examining regret and you come to learn its particular pain and fit yourself around it, so perhaps sometimes you hardly notice it at all. Regret can power your telescope, changing what you see.

Once you have felt regret, it has been in you and you have been in it and this does not change. It is like virginity that way.

Just as you would pull your hand away from something hot, the instinct is to withdraw but this is regret's strength, the relentless chase it gives; and it always wins.

But there is one way to feel less regret over the things that have happened in your life.

Through gratitude and humility.

Every assault, each transgression, all of the offenses, mistakes, and horrors. Because in truth, each was utterly essential in creating the person who sits now on the other side of this page.

I am speaking now about recycling on the molecular level. I am speaking of looking at all you were given in exchange for a single mugging.

You survived. Other people who were mugged did not, but you did.

You came to understand fear. Now, if somebody you knew were assaulted, the things you said would be the things that mattered most for them to hear; your compassion becomes wider exponentially.

Consider the bounty of your dead. All the people you have

lost in your life have taught you what value is. They taught you how rare it is to breathe, how unbearably beautiful and sacred it is to feel an ache in the center of your heart.

Think of all that has happened. Each hurt has held you back in life. And now swim under the hurt and deeper, beneath the limitations these past events have imposed on you.

If you are betrayed, focus on what you learned, not how you were fooled.

If you lose your home, focus on what you want your new home to feel like.

If you fall out of love, remember the love and not the fall. If all you focus on is the fall, the fall will swallow you because it will grow. Focus is water and sunlight. It causes growth.

Recalculate all the wrongs that have been done to you and examine the benefits that happened as a result of them. Be grateful for the bad things that happened and were in some way responsible for the good things that followed.

Did you catch that *be*?

Be. Thankful.

Because this one can slip right past you so easily.

Telling yourself you're thankful—"No, I totally get what you're saying and I really am grateful, you know, for a lot"—is not the same as *being* thankful. It's not the same as *feeling* that although betrayal hurts in the rudest, most brutal way, it does leave behind highly valuable knowledge in the form of experience. What you gain is larger and more valuable for your life as a whole than what you lost to betrayal. Because each betrayal is studied by your instincts. And human instinct is ancient and reliable, utterly mysterious and possibly capable of great genius. I believe that refined, fluent instincts are a person's most valuable asset. My own instincts have repeatedly guided me against the grain of logic and probability. When I have trusted and followed their direction, they have never been wrong. I don't know how or why. But I know that every significant experience—positive or negative—sharpens them and makes them more accurate.

Only by embracing all that you regret and not denying it, only by placing the highest value on what you've gained because of all you've lost, does regret lose the ability to cripple you.

II

It was difficult for her to speak, as though she hadn't spoken a word for many years and things had settled in her throat—things she wished she'd said, feelings she never expressed, her worst fears.

She coughed several times and when the words finally did arrive they were soaking wet.

"My son died two months ago from alcoholism. What is almost worse for me than losing Sean, that was his name, but what was almost worse than losing him is knowing that he died alone in his apartment, drunk. The loneliness he must have felt to drink himself literally to death." She paused here and I thought she might not continue but she did.

"When I think of it I can't think of it for very long or I feel like I will die, too. And yet, I can't stop going back there in my mind to his apartment to try and be with him. Even if I couldn't have stopped him from drinking that night, I could—*I would*—have just sat there beside him and held his hand while he . . ."

This was a comment from an audience member at one of

my book signings. The bookstore had printed flyers advertising my event. They read, SPEND A HILARIOUS EVENING WITH AUGUSTEN BURROUGHS.

The audience was silent and in suspense. Clearly, they felt terrible for this poor woman. It was possible the audience was also just a tiny bit thrilled that I was on the stage and not them; they would not have to say a word to the woman. I would.

I was quite eager to say something to her because I had already heard the un-truth inside what she said and I knew that once I pointed to it, she would see it, too.

I couldn't cut her off; I had to let her finish telling me. And the instant she fell silent, I asked, "Ma'am, how old was your son? How long had he been drinking?"

It was not the response she had expected, if she had expected anything. "He was twenty-five. He'd been struggling with alcohol since he was fourteen but his father and I didn't know about it until he was eighteen."

"Okay," I said. "So he was an alcoholic for more than half his life. I mean, it's not like this guy picked up a bottle one night and drank himself to death; he had a long history of heavy drinking. Right?"

All she did was nod.

"Yeah. Well, I'm very sorry you lost your son, I'm sorry he died. But I can tell you as an alcoholic myself, your son probably had a wonderful death. When you've been drinking that long, it takes a tremendous amount of alcohol to take you to 'that place' that you need to reach. And when you are there, inside of that drinking night, even if you are lonely, it is a very familiar, almost comfortable kind of lonely. And when you are that drunk, it is just impossible to explain how wonderful it can feel, the complete oblivion. I mean, there is a reason most alcoholics will not recover. It feels good, even as it ruins your life.

"I can tell you that I have woken up with lacerations, in terrifying locations with completely unfamiliar and unappealing people; but all of it was an adventure, when I was doing it. So I think the chances are, your son was engaged in some elaborate drunk fantasy and then he passed out and that was it. It is terrible and very sad that your son didn't want to get sober, but it is a fact that he did not because ultimately, he preferred being drunk.

"Which means, your son died doing what he loved most in the world. And I think there is no possible better death than to die while you are doing something you love above all else."

The woman clutched the wad of tissues in her hands and brought them both to her mouth. "Oh my God," she said.

And I thought, "Oh, fuck. She totally doesn't understand what I said."

Then the words escaped her as though a valve had burst and carried the words on a jet of air. "I never thought of it like that. I never did."

"I am right about this. I almost died alone in my apartment from drinking. Your son was in the same place but then he kept going. I can also tell you, he sure as hell wouldn't have wanted his mom sitting there holding his hand or whatever. You know? You did all you could do; you gave birth. Beyond this, it's up to him. It really and truly is. I don't mean to devalue the role of the parent but, speaking from my own experience, thank God parents aren't actually a necessity."

The thing is, you just wouldn't think on the face of it that there was any deeper truth to be found beyond the facts as she laid them out.

But they were objective facts; they were remote. What mattered to her was her son and his suffering.

The fact she was missing was *his* fact. He loved alcohol. He died doing what he loved most.

I still think about this woman, all these years later. I wonder if she has found any comfort at all in what must be life's most uncomfortable place. I wonder, too, if she continues to be eaten by regret, by thoughts of wishing she'd been with him or if she was able to see that the experience was so very different for her son than for her.

And I hope she does not live in a dark world. Because even the most terrible loss doesn't have to make you darker; it can make you deeper.

How to Stop Being Afraid
of Your Anger

ANGER IS PRETTY MUCH considered a trashy emotion that modern, civilized people can choose not to feel; they can "rise above" it by taking a number of deep breaths, thinking about something positive, and then moving on.

By ignoring anger and applying a thick coating of positive thinking on top of it, you can successfully contain it. Until, that is, the most inappropriate moment imaginable where your anger will roil up inside of you, rise up your throat, and be propelled out of your mouth at a pregnant woman who reaches for the avocado at the same moment that you do at farmers' market on some Saturday morning.

In my experience, people frequently repress small pieces of anger: office indignations, various slights, something hurtful a partner says or does. These little angers are swallowed and gulped down at the moment they are perceived.

Because, it doesn't matter. Or, they didn't mean it. Or, I'm overly sensitive. Or, I want to focus on the positive. Or a thousand and twelve other reasons.

But these little angers are promiscuous; they breed like epidural addicts. And in time, you're sitting across from your husband at dinner and when he opens his mouth to take a bite of garlic bread, you clench your teeth, smile, and think to yourself, "I despise the way he chews. How could I have married a man who chews like such an animal?"

Anger that you *shush* will metastasize and can cause massive damage to yourself, your life, and those around you. Anger that remains unvented can lead to depression, suicide, and other self-destructive behaviors. If anger isn't correctly processed and expressed in a productive fashion, raw, unrefined, 100 percent natural anger can result in murder.

Anger is a natural emotion, not a character flaw and not a weakness. But unlike joy or sadness, anger needs just a little bit of a polish before you release it into the world.

Even though it's horribly uncomfortable, you could try expressing how you feel to the subject of your wrath. "Alisa, I don't want to make a big deal out of this or anything, but I'm feeling . . . ? Like, the anger? At you because I just think you should have told me you were dating my dad." You can even use California art-college up-speak if it makes communication easier for you.

Another quite useful and healthy outlet for anger is writing. Even if you "can't write." Because actually, if you can speak, you can write. It's just a period of adjustment using your fingers instead of your mouth. But if you write—or type—exactly what you're thinking, without even a single change, when you read it, whatever you wrote will sound like you, talking. That's writing. No MFA required. Especially if what you're going to write is a letter. This is exactly the method you should use to express anger at people like your boss. You can write your letter immunity-from-prosecution style so you don't need to be rational or reasonable or even justified in your anger. You can just cut loose and wish them under the wheels of a bus with one thousand beautiful words.

Just don't send it.

The difference between writing the letter and sending it and writing the letter and not sending it is mental health.

Here's something about anger: if you are the kind of person who absolutely dreads anger and confrontation, you may have noticed that when you are involved in a confrontation where there is anger in the air, you may feel especially clear in your thinking. Even if you also feel withdrawn emotionally and say not a word.

Because anger can be clarifying. Anger isn't always irrational and blind, like rage—which is anger with the volume turned all the way to the right. Anger can serve to clarify how you feel in one sharp instant. With this clarity can come fuel.

Screenplays, novels, bodies of photographic work, sculpture, needlepoint, films—all of these forms of art can be fueled on ordinary, everyday, unleaded anger.

When I was a teenager, I was in a state of almost constant rage. Rage is so energizing that it makes your face warm. Rage is the stuff of double homicides, high school shootings, courthouse bombings. Rage cannot be directly expressed with good results.

While anger is often clarifying, rage mined directly from the earth of your emotions is the opposite. Hence the moniker *blinding.*

Rage needs to be mixed with an alkaline, like pen and paper, or third-person-in-the-room-with-a-degree-in-psychotherapy.

Rage is also honest. When you feel rage, there is no doubt that you have reached the rock-bottom truth of how you really feel. This is what makes rage something not to fear or try desperately to crush back, but to express. And to express it in a way that puts its phenomenal power to the best possible use.

It was a moment of pure rage that I experienced when I was living in a slum in Western Massachusetts, on my own at seventeen, in poverty and watching my father—who had just paid me a visit—drive away from my building. Our exchange triggered a rage so fully consuming that the choice I made in that instant—to succeed at something—was fueled until I made it to California and got my first real job several years later.

That's the other thing: eventually, you're going to want to stop for gas. Because you can fan a burning rage by never questioning it or reexamining it. It'll keep you fueled. But it will also keep you angry.

You will be an angry person.

You will hate a lot of things.

You will punch walls. You will be that person who snaps insanely, out of context, over the smallest things at work or in line at the supermarket.

Harboring a chest filled with rage year after year wears you away. It grinds you down until you are all nerves and bone.

You need to get rid of it. This is where rage is a lot like physical obesity: the treatment is similar. The more rage you contain, the harder you need to work physically.

And by "work" I do not mean "emotional work" as in therapy; I mean work as in housework, lawn work. Bench presses at the gym, gymnastics, a trapeze class.

Smart people sometimes feel like they are "of the mind" and not of the body, so they pay perhaps less attention to this area of their lives. But even Einstein was a sack of meat.

Rage is associated with a low serotonin level. Exercise cranks up the levels of this neurotransmitter. The effect is soothing.

When you live with very old, still-too-hot-to-touch anger, it fucks with you by making you feel rotten inside. By rotten, I mean decayed. I mean foul. I mean ruined. So much anger over so long a period makes you believe that somewhere along the way, you got broken and now you don't work anymore. It's a powerful emotion that endures, it can seem like a part of you. But it's not. It's a feeling, just like *surprise*. It's neurons in your brain and neurotransmitters in your blood. A kickboxing class is good for you, mechanically. Psychologically, what helped me was to not allow rage to be blind and anonymous, but to know its source.

And then get on with it. Because tracing an emotion to its root cause doesn't mean you then go and mentally move back into the past and live with it.

Also, you have to try to be nice enough for somebody to like you enough to be willing to rub your back.

Pissed-off people need back rubs and they also need gym memberships.

How to Be Sick

I

SOME PEOPLE MISUNDERSTAND THE phrase, "nothing worth having comes easy." They think it means hard work. Like, if they get into the office an hour before everyone else and they don't mess around online they'll be rewarded with The Good Things in life.

It has nothing to do with hard work.

What that phrase really means is, the most valuable moments and experiences that life has to offer are found only along its most treacherous paths.

"Nothing worth having comes easy" is not about showing up early at the office. It's about showing up in your own life. And living inside the very moment you want to run away from.

Your husband goes to the doctor because of a rash. The doctor tells him he has cancer of unknown origin.

On Tuesday your girlfriend is bored out of her mind. On Wednesday she's told she has MS.

How could you survive such news?

II

The day of diagnosis will seem like the end of your life and the beginning of your death. Now, instead of a future when you contemplate what's next, you will see only a large gray CAT scan machine blocking your view of the terrifying unknown behind it.

The first thing you must understand is that when something is new the novelty or newness itself carries weight. This makes the message weigh more.

Bad news is even worse when you are first told of it.

The diagnosis will never be as terrifying as it is the first day it is given to you.

Because you must also bear the weight of surprise.

New things occupy more volume than the laws of physics should allow. Just place a single new object in your living room and let the dog in. The new object is the only thing the dog will see.

The day of the diagnosis will be terrible and overwhelming. The day after will be less so. But before I take you through some very specific, real-life, cut-to-the-chase truths, I have to tell you the single, overriding, deepest truth about disease. And it's true no matter what the diagnosis: once you're in it, it's okay.

Often, when you receive a diagnosis, you will be given a prognosis as well. The prognosis may be uselessly vague or horrifyingly specific. There may be features of your disease that are simply too awful to contemplate. Or very little information at all.

In disease, it is the *anticipatory stress* that causes much of the suffering and anxiety. Thinking *about* something that could happen to you is always worse than when the very thing you dread actually happens. When it does, you are surprised to see that it's okay.

I paid with more than six years of my life to learn this particular truth. Had I known it from the beginning, I would have gained those years instead of losing them. I'm going to say it again because when you read it the first time, it almost sounds like I'm saying, "You'll be okay." And that's not what I'm saying. It looks like that's what I'm saying if you read it too fast.

Once you're in it, it's okay.

Whatever it is. However bad it gets. It won't be the way you imagine it will be from where you stand now. It won't be anything like what you imagine right now. It will be more like *today* than the way you think it will be.

As a matter of fact, it will be exactly like today. Except, not exactly the same elements will be in place.

It is always easier to have six days left to live than it is to be *told* you have six days left to live. This is the fundamental and profound truth of illness.

The difference is, living in the moment versus living in a state of obsession about how many moments remain.

One of the things I dreaded most was the possibility that at some point in the future, George could become so sick that he would be completely unable to work. He could require twenty-four-hour-a-day nursing care. He could be attached to IV lines and have to have a pole beside him, even when he went to the bathroom. He could even end up with one of those ghoulish, awful chest tubes. And if he ever became this sick, the vigorous, outdoor-loving man that I knew could be rendered into a shell of a man, unable to even leave his home. Unable to drive, unable to go outside for a walk. No longer able even to walk his own dog. The thought of this healthy man being plunged into such a useless and pitiful life was almost more than I could bear.

When everything I dreaded did come true, and the nurse installed the tubes, George wanted to watch a movie that was on TV. I had thought we would talk about the tubes or "deal" with the tubes. But there was nothing to deal with. Suddenly, there were tubes. And there was a movie on. We watched the movie. He was connected to tubes. It was fine. Tubes never mattered. George no longer worked and could not leave the house. I wouldn't have noticed this unless I paused to realize it. We were so busy with a life that certainly would have looked horrifying to anybody peering through the window.

III

I had spent all those years dreading what were now the best times we'd ever shared. It was awful. Not being able to even take a walk cannot be spun into something positive. But it didn't matter. And that's the truth. It didn't matter at all that he couldn't go outside. We had all we needed inside. It was very warm and comfortable there, in the heart of the fatal disease. I hadn't expected that.

The day of diagnosis will be overwhelming, frightening,

and confusing. The first thing you will do when you get back home will be to Google the name of the disease. Here you will read many terrifying things, but also some very hopeful things, perhaps.

You'll see certain features of the disease that are quite sobering and that you think might be best kept to yourself. That's a good instinct: *do keep it to yourself.*

When you are the partner of somebody diagnosed with something, you are codiagnosed automatically as a Disease Bride. Because Disease Brides are not the ones with the disease, they have room to carry additional information about complications, uncommon side effects, worst possible outcomes.

As the Disease Bride learns about the condition on this first day, he or she will experience a thickening of the brain. There will be a point when no additional information can be absorbed. The reason for this is far too obvious to be apparent: you will be learning a new language now, in the style of the Berlitz Total Immersion method. One week from the day of diagnosis and you will find it difficult to believe there was ever a time when you did not know what a tumor marker was.

The next several days will be intense and emotionally exhausting for both of you and for everyone else in the household.

But already there is good news: while it may seem the days are getting heavier and more overwhelming, this is optical illusion. Ninety percent of everything you read or hear is unfamiliar. When something is unfamiliar, you shield your face from it, you try to shove it back. But very soon after diagnosis, you will learn that information about the disease is not something to fear or run from. Information is your friend. You will come to crave much more information than is available.

These first couple of weeks you will be on the long, steep

ramp that leads to the highway. This is where you have to learn the fundamental features of the disease and understand what this disease means in the context of your life. Better to know there is the possibility of sudden blindness than to wake up blind and surprised. And absolutely, this will be overwhelming, stressful, frustrating, and utterly confusing and contradictory. In other words, this is Satan's medical school.

But this initial, getting-to-know-you/getting-to-know-all-about-you phase is transient and not a new facet of your life. You will never feel as overwhelmed and over your head as you do now.

During this time, there may likely be additional tests to confirm or rule out various possibilities, and available treatment options may be discussed or even begun. Each visit to the doctor should result not only in more information about the disease but a prescription for antiwrinkle face creams, high-potency pain relievers, muscle relaxers, and other luxury or life-cushion medications.

You may be forced to make choices without enough time or information to feel confident in the decisions you make. This is a new and permanent architectural feature of your life.

Confidence is rarely encountered and will almost never be felt in any medical context.

Everything will always happen too fast, or not fast enough. This is Disease Standard Time and it moves much faster than Eastern, Central, Mountain, or Pacific Standard Time. Unless, of course, it moves much slower or does not appear to move at all. More on this in a moment. Early on, get the cell phone number and personal email of every doctor who will be caring for you. Nobody attends medical school so they can leave the office behind at five and enjoy a peaceful evening scrapbooking.

Never abuse your access to your physician; never hesitate to contact her if you have a real, non-Internet-solvable issue.

After the initial shock of diagnosis and the overwhelming information overload of the ramp-up and any additional diagnostic procedures are complete, you, your newly diagnosed loved one, and your new disease will be alone together.

What happens now?

Your life happens now.

With disease, it's strictly Pay As You Go. What affects you now is what you deal with now. We never overpay disease.

This means, if one of the possible issues you may face is a loss of motor skills or even paralysis, know that these may at some stage be features of your own disease but until they are, they are not. So, a twitching in the pinkie is not the shuttle bus to paralysis and a feeding tube. A twitching in the pinkie is only a twitching in the pinkie and this remains true for as long as it is true.

Pay only for what you use. Accept one's current state as one's new default and move forward. If last week your diseased loved one's vision was fine but this week it is compromised, accept the compromise as the new default. It may be temporary, it may not. It may get worse, it may not. The sooner you are able to accept new features of your disease and not resist with denial, the sooner you will experience the single blessing of sickness: once you're in it, it's okay. But you must be in it. You cannot live in a state of refusal. You must accept what's happening now; know what could happen tomorrow but never accept tomorrow's possible disease feature before it arrives.

In diseases that qualify you for handicapped license plates and parking stickers, get these now. Never mind that not having them makes you feel normal. "Normal" in this context is a lie: it means "prediagnosis." With Disease is your new normal. As part of your compensation package for taking on disease, you are owed easy parking for the rest of your life. Shaving four minutes off walking from your car into the mall might seem ridiculous right now but there may come a day when those four minutes are needed on the backend. Those four minutes could end up feeling like the very thing all the other minutes of your life were leading up to. So get the sticker and the plates and use them.

IV

Nothing is ever as bad as you anticipate it will be. Even the worst thing you can imagine is not so terrible when viewed from the inside. Because *once you are inside it, it's okay.* Be aware of the potential worst. But don't accept it in advance.

The reason is that it may never arrive and so we must never overpay the illness. Current symptoms should be understood to contain the potential to improve or stay the same.

Accept this state of fluctuation. The feeling of frustration one encounters when speaking to medical personnel is usually the result of "trying to get a handle on this disease," to "know what to expect." This is merely a coy rephrasing of one's natural desire for structure and definition. It is only human to seek facts that can then be used to construct a sense of definition, if not certainty. But disease requires we live our lives fully and well, inside of the moment currently at hand and beneath the umbrella of uncertainty.

Part of accepting disease is accepting that any or all of its potential features may apply to you at some point. This means facing the possibility of some frightening physical changes.

But once we are diagnosed, we are within the disease. It is not an option now to return to a previous state of being. There is no "before" and there is no "after" because there exists only now.

Before and after, then and tomorrow are ideas. They are concepts. These places do not actually exist until they do. Nobody wants severe symptoms. Nonetheless, they do occur.

It is best to be aware that they may happen to you. Once diagnosed, you are automatically and irrevocably now one of the "other people." These are the people who experience the awful things you, yourself, are immune from. So, while cancer may have once been something that happens to "other people," now you are one of the other people. Anything can happen to you.

In order for this to not be extremely terrifying, it is essential to understand what I told you before: even severe symptoms are not as severe when you are inside of them. Just as your car has airbags you never see during the course of normal, uneventful automotive ownership, so too does your human self contain a powerful ability to adapt that you may be entirely unaware of until this ability is activated within you.

This is a fact: never "hope" you don't get certain later-stage symptoms. When you "hope" not to get a set of symptoms, you automatically empower those symptoms. If hair loss appears to be inevitable, allow the hair loss to arrive but do not give the hair loss a police escort and a parade to make its arrival that much more impactful.

Hoping one will avoid certain symptoms never prevents

the symptoms. It only makes the possibility of their arrival all the more terrifying by infusing them with the parade of dread.

If one day a new symptom appears, you will adjust and the new symptom will no longer be new. It is the unknown that we are compelled to fear and dread. It is the unknown that we see as the enemy.

Once you are inside any given set of symptoms, they become a familiar part of you and the fear is drained away and replaced with the task of coping. It's just like how if somebody showed you a photograph of your clean home as it would appear if occupied by a curious, energetic, uncoordinated, and filth-adoring two-year-old, you might very well decide that goldfish and not children would better suit your lifestyle. But if you have such a two-year-old and your house is currently in such a state of chaos, the mess is probably the last thing you care about.

V

You are not moving into a new gated community where everything you know will now change. This is not a new lifestyle. You have not just purchased your first home beside a lake in Cancertown or AIDS Point. It is only a disease.

And it becomes ordinary very fast.

And it remains ordinary for as long as you live.

So, do not become a couple with MS who still finds time for a dinner out. Be the busy couple that eats out frequently but is able to work MS into their schedule. This is what works best. I know, I have done it both ways.

VI

Never sit at the kitchen table dipping crusty sourdough into olive oil and talking "realistically" about "how bad this could really get."

Disease does all the work for you. It was designed for the lazy.

Your disease will inform you of what to worry about, when.

Furthermore, two people with the same disease may face very different issues. If Jan went blind two months after diagnosis, this does not mean you should be online shopping for braille flash cards. Likewise, if Jan experienced pain in her lower lip before she went blind, experiencing pain in your own lower lip does not mean you will now go blind as well.

Only when a feature of the disease presents itself should that feature be incorporated into your life.

There will always be new materials to read with respect to the disease. These will always be helpful unless they are frustrating. Either way, both the person with the disease and their Disease Bride should take lots of naps and have lots of snacks.

When it all feels so daunting and confusing, dramatic and horrible, when you feel like, why even try?

Take a nap. Naps are especially helpful during the overwhelming initial ramp-onto-the-highway phase.

Knowledge is important but naps are more important. The details of treatment are often confusing. Cheese is easy to understand. Eat cheese.

It helps to reward yourselves with things like real butter and cupcakes. Looks like both legs will have to be removed next Thursday? That means buttercream frosting. The doctor would like to review some lab results with you?

If he is willing to go over the results on the phone: French fries.

If he insists on seeing you in person: cheese fries.

Don't forget to always have soup on hand. Bad news should be followed with soup. Then a nap.

Fight each new horror with an even richer treat.

Why nobody tells you this is a great mystery: on the day you have a blood transfusion, a grilled cheese sandwich will be the best you have ever had.

If the ability to walk is lost, brownies will taste better.

This is a fact.

The person who loses their ability to walk will care more about the brownies than about the walking. Because if they have lost the ability to walk, they have accepted the loss. Walking was then, brownies are now.

You would be amazed by what you can give up, lose, or break and yet still be a person who gets happy over brownies.

It only *seems* like I am kidding.

VII

When concerned friends ask if there's anything you need, the answer they expect is, "No, we're doing okay."

This has two effects: the person who is concerned and would like to help but doesn't know how continues to do nothing and you do not have a casserole dish of scalloped potatoes sitting on the counter. So when friends or family members ask if there's anything they can do, suggest that they make from scratch the very best thing they make from scratch, then drive on over, open the door, and place the food inside. They can then turn around and head home because nobody at your house has the energy to even say hi.

The person will absolutely love this suggestion. Especially the part where they don't have to see the sick person. Nobody knows what to say to somebody who suddenly has stage-four ovarian cancer. It's exactly the same as announcing to your friends that you have taken a second husband and that the three of you will now be living under the same roof.

Your friends naturally have a thousand questions but not one of them seems appropriate to ask.

But not asking will create emotional distance. It's better to ask. When walking into the sick room of the diseased, instead of saying, "Hi Julie, oh my gosh, those are lovely flowers," you could say, "Hi Julie, so if you could improve one thing about this setup here, what would it be?"

Maybe there's something you really could improve.

GRATITUDE IS ESSENTIAL. "THANK you disease hammer for giving me brain cancer instead of —————————————."

"Thank you disease hammer for giving me ALS *after* I lost my virginity."

"Thank you disease hammer for giving me a variant of ALS that does not prevent the swallowing of vanilla pudding."

There is always something for which you can be extremely grateful.

Even if the disease progresses with relentless speed. Even if suddenly, you sense that death has slipped into the room with you.

. . .

ONE DAY YOU MAY find yourself lying on the bed beside the person you love. Both of you inside of disease. Perhaps you will be watching the liquid slowly rise in a column within a straw.

Maybe you both have been at this for a while. But now, even drinking from a straw is almost too exhausting.

The water rises, reaches the neck where the straw bends like an accordion, but then so suddenly it falls back down into the glass again.

Until, as you watch in such suspense you actually hold your own breath, and the water loops into the bent neck of the straw and into their mouth. Because you know this person so well, even though they say not a single word, you can read in their eyes exactly what's on their mind. "See? Five bucks, cough it up and then hand me back my life."

When death arrives, it will arrive in its coach: death rides the last breath in.

There is no exhale.

THIS MAY BE THE moment—it is for many—that what has been given to you will be unwrapped.

You see, dying is not the same as dead. Going is not yet gone. Dead is dead and it is unmistakable. Death does not resemble peace; it resembles gone.

When the person you love is gone, even if it has seemed to you for so long only a small part of them has remained, you see now how much of them was really there. You see, too, that it was the last few moments—hardly enough of them to walk from the far end of a parking lot to the front door of a mall—and yet these several moments were the most pure, most essential, and most *alive* moments in your life.

When you reflect on the water rising in the straw, you will see now what you missed then because you were there, inside the straw, inside the moment, inside the disease: that was the closest you have ever been to another person. One person can be no closer to another.

As the liquid flowed into their mouth and you saw a tiny shine of wet and felt their joy at the achievement of a single sip, you had become as close as two people can be.

Life tucks its rarest, largest, and most D-flawless diamonds deep, deep inside the folds of the greatest loss. You do not know they are even there, glittering in the dark, right beside you.

When you reach the very interior moments of the end—a tiny breath, one flash of the person you love in their eyes, just the fluttering of eyelashes—these are the diamonds that will shine all the way into the future, for as long as you are alive.

These last moments, diamonds: the hardest thing known to man. But, too, the most brilliant, the most extravagant, and utterly worth whatever price we had to pay to have them.

How to Lose Someone
You Love

I

I KNEW A WOMAN who was approaching forty and had not yet experienced the death of anybody close to her.

She had never even attended a funeral.

She told me once, "I guess I've been really fortunate in that way."

But when she said this, it may have been the first time she had ever considered aloud her status as a virgin of another sort.

Because I saw something like a shadow pass over her face, as if she were standing beneath a very low and quickly traveling cloud. And I think it might have been her realization that the good fortune she had experienced of never losing someone would end.

She perhaps saw that her luck in this regard was finite.

She had not escaped this loss. It had only been delayed.

But there is nothing a person can do to prepare for the death of someone close.

I tried this and it backfired.

I loved somebody with a terminal illness. What I did was try and love them not quite so hard; I tried to need them less.

In the hope that I could more evenly distribute the weight of loss.

As such, their death was on my mind for years before they died.

It was as if I made eggs and arrangements in the same black iron skillet.

II

When they died I saw instantly that I had failed entirely to lessen the impact of loss. I had instead overpaid for death by living so long with the idea of it in my mind, planning for its arrival, making sure the sheets were fresh.

I learned that the proper way to prepare for someone's death is by being alive in the same room with them for as long as you are allowed.

III

There are two kinds of death: the good death and then every other death.

In a good death, there is time.

And the dying person retains their mental clarity.

Sometimes a good death will be a great one and there will

be many days for you to spend together. You will be able to say good-bye. Maybe even use that word. In a great death, people do not pretend they don't know why there is a morphine drip in the room. In a great death, no one is afraid to say the word *dying.*

But a great or a good death is not something you are allowed to ask for or expect. Planes do go down. Hearts do suddenly stop. People are alive and then without any prior notice they are not.

In this case, you will struggle to say good-bye but because good-bye is by nature a mutual affair, the good-bye will be only one-sided. Necessary but so terribly hollow.

IV

If the death is a good death, there will be a bed.

And the bed will be the world.

It may be at home or in a hospital. It may be that the bed is not located where you want it to be and this can be cause for tremendous distraction and upset.

"But dad should be at home in his own bed."

Know this: as death itself approaches, it does not matter where the bed is located because the bed is all there is.

In a good death, people who love the dying person will be clustered near or even on top of the bed. A hand or a leg will be in constant contact with the dying loved person.

Off the bed is where the unessential falls; it's where you dump your jacket, let the papers slide, reach for something to bring to the bed. In death, the bed is the very center of life; anything off the bed is merely in orbit.

It's hot there in the center.

You may feel feverish. But your hands will not sweat, they will remain clammy.

Even if you hold out hope for a miracle, if the person is in fact dying, you will know this. Though you may be unable, just yet, to allow this to be true.

In this case, you will find you have many things to do: people to call, supplies that must be purchased. It will feel like you have taken over as the CEO of a company in chaos. But you will not mind these tasks; instead, you will feel grateful for them.

This is where a large error is easy to make: every moment you spend texting somebody an update or attending to other such clipboard tasks is a moment that will in time be seen as *more* lost from your life than any others.

Only from the great height of perspective much later will you understand that those last moments with the person you loved were among the most cherished moments of your life and it will feel special, like a brief holiday, to recall them.

So I will tell you now: spend as many moments as you possibly can with the dying person you love. It is not necessary to do anything or say anything. It is plenty to sit in the same room and feel drowsy.

It's difficult to do this.

If you sit still, you may be overwhelmed with the most terrible feeling that everything is spinning out of control, wildly so.

This is why it will be a relief to make calls or run petty errands that you normally would avoid. These things provide an artificial relief, a sense that you are "managing" the death.

It is better to realize and accept what is true: the feeling that everything is spinning out of control comes from the fact that it is.

We have no control over anything large in life; only the small details are under our direct management. But even then, we lack any real authority.

We can move the paper clips around on top of the desk, but what is the desk? And how did it get there? And will it be there tomorrow? We don't know.

V

As the moments progress further still and your loved person transitions from sitting upright to lying down, and from lying down to curling up, when death is very near, something happens to time: the minutes themselves suddenly expand and develop the ability to absorb more activity.

The quality of each moment will be raised to an impossibly high level. Sometimes, a single one can contain more substance than even an hour.

At the same time, these moments will pass much faster than they ever have before.

Never glance at a watch. Never look at the time.

Death, when it finally arrives, does so in a surprising fashion: it adds nothing to the room, not a light or a spark or a sound; death does not stir a molecule of the air.

You know it arrives because there is suddenly a subtraction. You will feel it before you know it.

When you look down at the person you have so carefully loved, you will see only their body and all that remains of them will be what remains in a pair of jeans stepped out of and left behind on the floor by the person who wore them.

If their death was a long and painful process you may have

come to believe that when the moment of death itself arrived, it would be, in some terrible way, a relief.

In which case the very first thing you are likely to feel is the simple stun of a slap across the face, the sting of truth: this is not a relief, not in even one microscopic way.

You will want to withdraw the thought from time.

Madly, it might even occur to you that doing so could possibly postpone what has happened by a very, very small though essential amount of time.

And your mind will crash into the wall of, but how?

You may cry very, very hard right now.

Even if you never felt there would be relief and you only tried to accept what was happening and experience the grace of the moments until the last one was there, the first thing you may feel now that the person you love is dead is that you weren't quite ready.

Possibly, you needed only ten more minutes. Maybe not even that much time. The amount you need will be utterly reasonable.

And therefore, doable.

You will occupy the same state of mind as if you were in line at the market and you stepped just ten feet from your place to grab a box of trash bags and when you turned around, somebody new had arrived and so you pry ahead of them with kind, polite authority and explain, "Hi, sorry. I'm actually here, I just had to step over there for this." Of course, in line the person nods and even feels a little embarrassed.

You will say, "I thought I was ready but I wasn't, you see. Just not quite ready."

But this is death. And they are dead.

You do not get your place back.

You may not have so much as one one-trillionth of a second with them. The door has closed and vanished into the wall and not even an outline of where it once was is visible.

Additionally, you may feel nothing at all. And if asked to describe how you felt, you might consider this and then reply, "I feel like off-white canvas."

Or you may feel as though the bottom, the floor of the world has given way and you are in a free fall.

VI

I wonder if there is a biological reason, one that is coded into our genetic profile, that requires us to experience fully the heavy pain of loss.

Because thrill and joy and triumph and achievement and orgasm and surprise—these things are so fleeting.

But grief endures.

If not all of us will ever know certain joys, we will know loss. It's as if at birth, a baby's foot is inked and stamped onto a contract in agreement of the terms: the price of life will be losing someone you love. Nobody remembers signing anything of the kind. Yet you cannot live a full, natural life without experiencing a full and natural death.

VII

It may seem to you that your life is over now. Your future without the person you love is no future at all.

Death is a head-on collision with your plans.

But everything in life—the gold fillings of your teeth, the cotton of your sheets, the air you breathe, all the food you will ever eat—everything there is was born from a collision.

Inside every single thing that lives is a debt to a distant star that died.

Nothing new is ever created without one thing colliding into another.

And something new is created when the person you love dies.

Because they are not the only ones who die: you die, too. The person you were when you were with them is gone just as surely as they are.

This is what you should know about losing somebody you love. They do not travel alone. You go with them.

How to Let a Child Die

I

WHEN MY AUNT IN Dothan, Alabama, lost her hair during her treatment for cancer, she did exactly the right thing: she shaved her head and posed near a motorcycle even though she, herself, would never ride a motorcycle.

This is exactly the right thing to do because it's exactly what a kid would do. If a kid woke up bald, a kid would want to *be* bald. That might include wearing a wig. But it would always be a wig on top of a bald kid. The kid would tell you this much.

When disease happens to kids, the parents wish it had happened to them instead. Many times, the parents want to know how God could allow their kid to get sick.

No matter your spiritual beliefs, if you hold any, the answer is the same: sometimes, *why* is not knowable.

If you open the refrigerator door and a tub of Kozy Shack tapioca pudding tumbles out and splats open onto the floor, you clean it. You don't stand there and question why it happened, how it was possible.

Why doesn't matter now.

Even though nothing in the world seems to matter except why. In fact, the desire to understand is so powerful that it feels almost like within the answer is salvation or rescue.

But it doesn't matter why, not at all.

Maybe it matters next time, for the next person. But not now, not for you.

Kids are diagnosed with terrible diseases every day, all over the world. This has happened for as long as we have populated the earth.

It may be the single worst thing that can happen to people—maybe to all mammals. Haven't you seen on one of the nature channels an image of a mama elephant standing above her dying baby elephant?

What's most heartbreaking about a child with a serious illness is not even how sick they become; rather it's how good at being sick children are.

And they are even better at dying.

Because children are made out of the truth. All untrue things a child believes are placed there by others.

So you shouldn't ever be afraid to be honest with your sick child. You will scare them much more by misrepresenting the reality. Kids know when adults are lying. And they don't like it.

But how can you, as a parent, even form the words, "Yes, you're dying," if your child asks you?

As you will one day discover for yourself, sickness, death, awfulness have little gifts inserted into them, just exactly at the right moment.

There is such a gift, albeit tiny. Smaller than the smallest thing you can think of. But that's large enough to be able to tell your child the truth, even if they are dying, without having to tell them they're dying.

II

But first, I must tell you again how small this is. It is not something you can ever wish for and I don't think I'd pray for it, either. It almost doesn't exist, except it does. Spontaneous remission is the term used by the medical community to describe what they cannot explain: the sudden, unexpected recovery from an illness or condition.

The nontechnical term is *miracle*.

Even if you do not believe in God, you must believe in miracles because there exists several hundred years' worth of careful—if puzzled—documentation on this medical phenomenon.

III

Imagine that your child is diagnosed with a terminal, stage-four cancer.

Perhaps you seek second and third opinions and each is identical: your child is dying. There is nothing we can do.

Now imagine that your certainly dying child is eleven or twelve and extremely smart and they ask you, "Am I dying?"

You have never lied to your child.

IV

If your child was terminally ill and they asked you, "Am I dying?" what would you tell them? Because maybe the only thing worse than lying to a child is lying to a child who's dying.

And what if they had that look in their eyes that seemed impossibly mature beyond their own few years and this look told you exactly, "We both know it, but you have to say it"?

Many children have an innate, preternaturally wise understanding of death. But because children are the very essence of vibrancy and life itself, it is nearly impossible for adults to believe that children could be such authorities of darkness.

All the children I have ever known were honest.

When they lie, it is a clumsy, transparent thing. The weight of the lie causes the edges of their fictional details to sag, exposing the seams.

Dishonesty is an embellishment, it is the gold plating that chips away. Dishonesty is learned behavior that becomes refined over many years.

So, what would you say to a dying child who asked you for the truth?

There are some parents who would want to salvage and protect what little time remains by telling their child, "You will be fine. It's hard right now, but the doctors are going to cure you." So that the child can spend the last of their time on earth doing things they love instead of spending this time making philosophical peace with their own mortality.

Other parents believe it is their duty to tell their child the painful truth if they are asked so directly. Because the child, knowing her time is now finite, may have certain things she would like to do before she's gone.

I believe that no parent can be faulted—indeed, can only be praised—for choosing either direction.

One choice is not necessarily better or more ethically correct than the other.

There is a third choice.

And I believe it is more technically correct than the other two. Therefore, I prefer it.

Throughout the history of medicine, there have been several—but not many—cases where somebody was diagnosed with a terminal illness and then became cured, quite suddenly and completely.

Although this medical phenomenon happens so rarely we can almost think of it as never occurring, the fact is it has and it does.

False hope is a cruel thing to give somebody. And talking about "spontaneous remission" to somebody who is dying is closer than spitting distance to giving false hope.

Except, it's not actually false.

Which is why even under the most dire medical circumstances, several molecules of hope should be kept in reserve.

And what do we know of anything, really?

I mean, *really*?

Maybe it's either resignation or assuredness that does you in. Maybe those who have not so much as a flicker of a spark of hope are the ones who spontaneously remiss, who become the meteorite that lands in the corner pocket of the pool table.

Too much hope is a delusion. Buying lottery tickets isn't optimistic; it's wasteful. Just as an absence of hope is an engineless plane that will glide *until*, but then no more.

But hope in a lean, trim, reasonable amount may very well be the primary ingredient of miracles.

In February 2009, *Scientific American* published an article about a 1957 medical case in which a man with advanced lymphoma was given a new and experimental cancer drug that was so effective, it shrank his tumors by more than half after only several days; he was discharged from the hospital shortly thereafter.

Except, this patient had been given the placebo form of the new and experimental cancer drug. Which is to say, the only active ingredient in this drug had been the man's own *hope*.

Those who were given the actual pharmaceutical showed no change.

Only the man who had been given nothing more than a little bit of hope had improved.

The placebo effect is a medically established fact.

What's not so well established is how it works.

Obviously, what we believe about our health can have a profound impact on it.

But in the absence of any hope, such as when a person is told there is no hope whatsoever for their condition, a similar though opposite phenomenon may occur: it is known as the nocebo effect.

The *nocebo effect* is the term used to describe the measurable, tangible, negative physical response that can occur when somebody is given a placebo and told that the "drug" will have harmful—instead of positive—effects.

While both the placebo effect and its dark-side evil twin are medically documented, clinically accepted facts, how either works is largely a mystery beyond simply saying, "Well, mind over matter is very powerful."

In the case of spontaneous remission, the majority of reported cases have eventually been attributed to either an inaccuracy in the initial diagnoses, so there was no cancer to begin with, for example—or fraud.

A handful of genuine examples remain. And they remain a mystery as well.

If spontaneous remission has happened, it can happen.

If only one butterfly's eyelash width of possibility exists that your terminally ill child might possibly, though almost certainly will not, wake up in the morning fully cured, does this alter what you might tell your own child if they asked you for the truth?

My feeling is, as long as something—anything, medical or otherwise—is within the realm of possibility, then there is hope.

Even if that for which we hope never comes to pass, I believe the experience of existing within a place of hope is an essentially, *elementally* richer and more valuable life experience than one in which all hope is entirely depleted.

In the early nineteenth century, a British explorer named Ernest Shackleton posted a notice in a British newspaper calling for men to serve as crew on his ship, *Endurance,* which he intended to captain through a trans-Antarctic expedition.

Twenty-eight men enlisted.

Endurance became trapped within drifting ice floats and was ultimately frozen in place. The crew soon realized they would remain frozen where they were until the ice melted, and this would not happen for nearly a year.

Shackleton managed and motivated his ice-bound crew for several months, until the ship was crushed by the ever-compressing ice.

Shackleton then led the men across the ice, propelled by their sled dogs. But the unimaginably brutal climate made reaching land impossible.

Ultimately, the salvaged lifeboats were loaded and these were used to deliver the malnourished, nearly-mad-with-despair crew to a small, bleak, barren island—more of a large rock, really—named Elephant Island. Here, the lifeboats were turned into shelters.

Shackleton had managed, against all odds and with seemingly no cause for any hope, to save the lives of his crew—but the land on which they now found themselves was entirely remote; rescue was not within the realm of possibility.

Taking his three strongest men with him, Shackleton set out to reach occupied land, where help could be found and the men remaining behind on Elephant Island could be rescued.

Although it would require seemingly superhuman navigational skills, impossible endurance, and then miraculous good fortune, Shackleton did reach the safety of land; and though it required not one, not two, but three separate attempts by ship, Shackleton would, four and a half months later, return as he had promised to Elephant Island and rescue his crew.

Despite the overwhelming odds against any of the men surviving a disaster of this magnitude, not a single crew member died.

These men had spent months living inside wooden lifeboats, which had been turned upside down into "shelters," on an island where there was not a single source of food and absolutely no reasonable expectation for rescue.

The single thing these men had was the word of their captain, who had promised to return for them.

So they subsisted on the reserves of their own body fat and just the smallest remains of food from their long-sunk ship.

And hope.

Hope kept them alive. And Ernest Shackleton saved their lives.

When he returned to England, he was knighted by King Edward VII.

If a photographer had not been among the crew and if these photographs had not survived, this entire story would be so absurdly against-all-odds that nobody would have believed it.

But the story of *Endurance* has always been for me the most perfect example of what hope is, what hope can do, and how there are times in life when logic and reason and probability must be recognized, but then ignored.

Miracles do happen.

You must believe this. No matter what else you believe about life, you must believe in miracles.

Because we are all, every one of us, living on a round rock that spins around and around at almost a quarter of a million miles per hour in an unthinkably vast blackness called space.

There is nothing else like us for as far as our telescopic eyes can see.

In a universe filled with spinning, barren rocks, frozen gas, ice, dust, and radiation, we live on a planet filled with soft, green leaves and salty oceans and honey made from bees, which themselves live within geometrically complex and perfect structures of their own architecture and creation.

In our trees are birds whose songs are as complex and nuanced as Beethoven's greatest sonatas.

And despite the wild, endless spinning of our planet and its never-ending orbit around the sun—itself a star on fire—when we pour water into a glass, the water stays in the glass.

All of these are miracles.

The gum stuck to the bottom of your shoe is a miracle of stratospheric proportions: that there is such a thing as *gum*, such a thing as a *shoe*, such a thing as a *human being*.

I mean, what are the odds?

Think of the actual physical elements that compose our bodies: we are 98 percent hydrogen and oxygen and carbon.

That's table sugar.

You are made of the same stuff as table sugar.

Just a couple of tiny differences here and there and look what happened to the sugar: it can stand upright and send tweets.

Because the sun seems yellow and friendly and we only notice the air when it stinks and we take all of this *existing* business entirely for granted, it's easy to forget or not even consider in the first place, not even once, that the fact that we exist, that we are a *we* at all, is the very definition of a miracle.

Miracle: an effect or extraordinary event in the physical world that surpasses all known human or natural powers and is ascribed to a supernatural cause.

It is simply a miracle that you woke up this morning.

And it is a miracle that, in billions of miles filled with blackness and rocks, you were born.

And if, against the odds of solar winds and burning stars and emptiness that extends for lifetimes, any single person could defy explanation and have the audacity to *be born*, then surely there must be at least one half of a tiny, tiny chance that the disease that is scheduled to kill your child will go entirely missing by morning.

While this may be so unlikely as to essentially be not within the realm of possibility, it is within the realm of possibility, but just.

"Daddy, am I dying?"

"Mom? Am I gonna die?"

"Yes, my love, the single immovable fact of your life, the only thing anybody—me or all the doctors in the world or anybody who is an expert in anything and everything—the only known certainty about your life is that it will end. Yes, my love, you are dying. And so am I. And so is the doctor. Life is a process of dying."

"Yeah, but does the doctor say I'm dying now?"

"The doctor says you are."

"So, am I?"

"Well. You know when you look up at the sky at night and you see stars? And you know how if you keep looking without blinking you see more stars? And how if you *keep* looking even longer you see that the black sky is really made almost entirely out of stars that seem to extend back and back and back forever? The chance that you will live is about the size of just one small star out of every star you see."

"So, not very much of a chance?"

"Not very much of a chance, no."

"But maybe a little chance?"

"Maybe. A very little, tiny, tiny chance."

"Okay."

How to Change the World by Yourself

I

I MET A BLACK MAN who told me about growing up in the
South when all the busses carried signs that told him to sit
in the back. As long as your skin color was the darker color
that people come in, you wouldn't sit in the front. The front of
the bus was for the people who made the laws and owned the
world and would turn red if they got mad.

WHITES ONLY is what the sign up front read.

He said, "That's just the way it was."

II

But there was one girl who questioned *the way it was*.

She was a black girl.

She couldn't sit in the front with the paler people, the whites.

If you even tried, probably a lot of them would look at you and they would turn that mad red color.

Back then if you were a black girl there just wasn't much less you could be.

But this girl saw something that either nobody else saw or folks saw but didn't think about. Or they thought about it but didn't say anything.

She saw that the world was broken.

Because, if you had coloring to your complexion, you could be called such horrible things.

She'd learned in school about the slavery. Which wasn't allowed anymore. But when it was allowed, the black people were like the animals. And the white people owned them and could make them do anything they wanted them to do.

But that was in the past so it was gone.

Except it wasn't. What if she wanted to sit in the front of the bus and see what it felt like? Maybe it was a bumpier and more fun kind of ride.

Or, maybe it was smoother and better for napping.

Maybe she wanted to sit in the front where you could only be white because slavery was over now.

It wasn't allowed anymore for white people to make pets out of the black people and be horrible to them.

Or tell them where to sit.

You couldn't do that. It was wrong.

It was a broken thing.

It was a lie.

So Claudette Colvin, a fifteen-year-old schoolgirl, took a seat up front.

Then she refused to give up her seat to a white person and move to the back of the bus.

She did this before anybody else had done it. Or, if somebody else had done it, nobody knew about it. Because the trouble didn't happen until Claudette.

When she refused and refused and refused to give up the seat that was as surely hers as if God himself had handed it to her, the police came and they pulled her off the bus.

There was a trial. It was this trial that decided everyone could sit where they wanted to sit on a bus.

All the people who hadn't even thought about it, thought about it now.

Once somebody peels back the curtain and exposes the truth, it's like the truth gets bolder in the air. And it becomes brighter, like a light.

Nine months later Rosa Parks became famous for doing exactly what young Claudette had done before.

Rosa Parks is an American hero who was carefully chosen to take the political stand that she did.

Claudette was not a polished, experienced civil rights activist; she was just a fifteen-year-old girl who saw something nobody else chose to see and believed in the deeper truth of it enough to *not* take a stand when it was required by law that she do exactly that when a white person stepped on to the bus.

Fifteen. She was fifteen.

The truth for as long as she'd been alive was that she belonged in the back of the bus, where all the other black people sat and had always sat for as long as anybody could remember.

That was just the way it was.

When something happens every day it becomes normal and true.

If enough people believe in something, you wouldn't even think to question it.

Whites up front, coloreds in the rear. Let's all just get going so we can get home.

The truth behind "the truth" is what Colvin saw. And she would not unsee it, even when angry, red men stormed that bus—imagine how the whole bus must have rocked and creaked each time the officers shifted their weight.

They must have looked at her like she was dog shit on the bottom of a shoe.

She must have seen this in their eyes. And it must have been more terrifying than anything she had ever experienced.

She did not let go of her grip on what was true.

I imagine many people thought, when they read about the trial of this young girl in the papers and then just nine months later, the same business with that second woman, Parks: "Hell, if they start sitting up front, where does it stop? You know what I mean? These are ignorant, ignorant folk. Hell, average old nigger 'round here don't know whether to scratch a watch or wind his ass. I am not fooling with you. I mean, we start letting these folk sit up front with all of us, you know it is just a matter of damn time before one of them gets it in their cotton-pickin' head that he might go on and round up all his damn buddies and—well, shit. One of these fuckers could end up mayor of this city.

"Now, I'm gonna tell you something. This is no damn joke, what this Parks girl has gone and done. It's already started.

"You just imagine it. Imagine if one day, one of these coloreds, he decides to run for the Oval Office. And I know, I know that may sound far-fetched.

"But I am telling you, there could come a day when one of them makes a run for president of these United States.

"This could happen, buddy. This could indeed happen. And the white man, he could find himself underneath the rule of a black man.

"Right here in our country. That is what could happen because of that first damn little girl that made a fuss.

"I wonder if she even is able to comprehend that her actions could potentially change the fundamental reality of our nation."

III

My family is from the South. Because they were landowners, our family records go very far back.

That's how I learned that my ancestors purchased the first slaves that arrived in America.

I wonder what my ancestors would think if they knew that I never voted in a single United States presidential election until I was forty-three years old.

And I had to ask the nice old white lady how to do it.

The nice old white lady said, "You've never voted? Ever?"

I said, "No."

She said, "Well, it would be my privilege to show you how to vote." And as she led me across the tile floor she added, "But I cannot *tell* you how to vote. Because this is America. And we value liberty and freedom above everything else."

I said, "That really is the truth, isn't it?"

She made the "oh" mouth that old people make sometimes. And she said, "Oh, yes. It most certainly is the truth."

IV

I voted for the man who had two black girls for daughters.

And he won.

Right now, the most powerful thing you can be in the world is a black girl.

This makes me feel safe.

The world isn't broken anymore. Or at least not all the way broken.

Because one little girl saw something glimmer beneath the surface and she knew by the shine of it that it was the truth.

She believed what she saw with her own eyes. She knew what she saw was the truth because that's what the truth is, you see. The truth is the thing you recognize instantly, even if you've never seen it before. You know.

Your blood knows it. Even the air around you knows it.

Truth is not an opinion. It's a force like gravity.

It's the most valuable substance known to man.

When the police pulled her from the bus, she was forced to let go of her seat up front, but these uniformed men could not grab her words out of the air, so the truth was released, airborne, as she shouted, *"It's my constitutional right!"*

Even though no great wind came upon the crowd and there was no bolt of lightning, even though it did not change from day to night, everything now was different.

In the blink of an eye, in the scream of a girl, there had been a change to the fundamental reality of our nation.

"It's my constitutional right!"

She had seen the truth. She had spoken it out loud. And this unleashed it into the world.

The world changed.

Nothing you build on inaccuracy or mere hope or longing or lies or laws that oppose the nature of things can endure. When the wind comes in the form of a young teenage girl, it will all be blown away, down to the bedrock of what's real, what's true.

This is how.

This is how you survive the unsurvivable, this is how you lose that which you cannot bear to lose, this is how you reinvent yourself, overcome your abusers, fulfill your ambitions and meet the love of your life: by following what is true, no matter where it leads you.

THIS IS WHY

T HE CALCIUM IN YOUR bones came from a star. We are all made from recycled bits and pieces of the universe. This matters because origins matter.

For example, if you were born to a reigning monarch but kidnapped by the black market shortly after birth and sent to America where you were raised by painfully common, unremarkable people from Ohio, and when you were in your thirties working as a humble UPS driver, dignitaries landed their helicopter on the roof of your crummy apartment building and informed you of their thirty-plus-year search for you, His Royal Highness, the course of your life might change.

You know?

Our familial genetic origins—medical histories—inform us of medical conditions that exist in our families, and when we know about these specific conditions, we can sometimes take certain actions to prevent them.

Which is why I think it's important to consider that billions of years before we were students and mothers and dog trainers and priests, we were particles that came together to form into star after star after star until almost *forever* passed, and instead of a star what formed was life—simplistic, crude, miraculous.

And after another almost infinity, there we were.

This is why for you, anything is possible.

Because you are made of everything.